"Amazingly great advice! Every couple and especially every young person needs to have Ellie's book *The Debt Diet*. We're buying it for all of our children!"

> **—Pam and Bill Farrel**
> Authors, *Men Are Like Waffles,*
> *Women Are Like Spaghetti*

"Ellie has done it again. . . . A relevant and timely piece of work about an issue that is killing marriages and families. Her practical approach will result not only in 'Debt Loss,' but also 'Relationship Gain,' as couples apply these principles in their handling of debt and money."

> **—Dennis Rainey**
> President, FamilyLife

Books by Ellie Kay

How to Save Money Every Day

Money Doesn't Grow on Trees

Shop, Save, and Share

Heroes at Home

A Woman's Guide to Family Finances

The New Bride Guide

The Debt Diet

the DEBT DIET

·····AN EASY-TO-FOLLOW PLAN to SHED DEBT & TRIM SPENDING ··········

ELLIE KAY

America's Family Financial Expert®

BETHANY HOUSE PUBLISHERS

Minneapolis, Minnesota

Published by Bethany House Publishers
11400 Hampshire Avenue South
Bloomington, Minnesota 55438

Bethany House Publishers is a division of
Baker Publishing Group, Grand Rapids, Michigan.

Printed in the United States of America

Library of Congress Cataloging-in-Publication Data

Kay, Ellie.
    The debt diet : an easy-to-follow plan to shed debt and trim spending / by Ellie Kay.
        p.   cm.
    ISBN 0-7642-0001-1 (pbk.)
    1. Finance, Personal. 2. Consumer credit. I. Title.
    HG179.K3787   2005
    332.024'02—dc22   2004020195

For Steve Laube,
Agent, Editor, and Friend to our Family

ELLIE KAY is a bestselling, award-winning author, national radio commentator, and regular media guest as well as a gifted speaker. She is a graduate of Colorado Christian University with a degree in the management of human resources. She and her husband, Bob, a contract fighter pilot with a major aerospace corporation, have five children at home and two adult children and make their home in Southern California.

If you wish to contact Ellie Kay for speaking engagements, media, or seminars, she can be reached at:

Ellie Kay
% Speak Up Speaker Services
1614 Edison Shores Place
Port Huron, MI 48060
speakupinc@aol.com
E-mail: *ellie@elliekay.com*
Web Site: *www.elliekay.com*

table of contents

Introduction . . . 9

SECTION ONE: THINKING THIN

SECTION TWO: FISCAL FITNESS

SECTION THREE: FOREVER FREE

Introduction

Getting out of debt is like going on a diet. What do you do if you want to lose weight? You eat less and exercise more. This sounds simple, but most of us know it sure isn't easy. We wish there were another answer, an easier, less painful answer. But there isn't. Most experts agree: Diet and exercise are the only things that really work. The way to get out of debt is much the same—the only thing that really works is to spend less and save more.

One of the amazing discoveries I made in writing *The Debt Diet* was that the same disciplines that are required to achieve physical health are required for financial health as well. And just as there is always a "new" diet breakthrough, there is usually also something new to be learned when it comes to finances. But beware of "fads" and so-called "quick fixes."

Sure, there are always "new" and "improved" ways of looking at money. You can sign on with a for-profit financial counselor who promises the moon. You can try to win the lottery. Or fall prey to a get-rich-quick scheme. But if you spend more than you make, you're still going to be in debt. And you won't be there alone.

Research by the Federal Reserve indicates: "Household debt is at a record high relative to disposable income. Some analysts are concerned that this unprecedented level might pose a risk to the financial health of American households." Is debt putting your household—your marriage—at risk?

In his bestselling book *Debt-Free Living*, Larry Burkett says, "It is interesting that the increase in the American divorce rate can be tracked on a curve matching the growth of debt in this country." Debt doesn't benefit a marriage or a family and it certainly doesn't benefit your future. Just as being overweight leads to health and emotional concerns, so debt has its consequences as well. You may want to consider the following:

- Debt puts your marriage at risk.
- Debt makes you a servant to the lender.
- Debt borrows from your future.
- Debt hinders sharing with others.
- Debt erodes resources through high-interest payments.

On the other hand, if you have a low debt load, you will experience many benefits. You will have the ability to give generously in order to meet the financial needs of others. You and your spouse will argue less over money. You will not be anxious over floating bills to pay minimums. You can confidently answer your phone instead of using your answering machine to screen calls from creditors. And you will avoid the stigma and burden of bankruptcy.

Getting out of debt may be easier than you think, even for major debt, such as a mortgage. Sometimes we quit before we start because the task seems far too great. If you have to lose fifty pounds, you concentrate on the first five pounds, not the entire amount!

Bob and I have experienced the incredible miracle of overcoming seemingly insurmountable debt. When we got married, we had $40,000 in consumer debt. Like many young people, we didn't realize the price we would pay for instant gratification.

We decided to get out of debt and made immediate changes in our lifestyle to accomplish this. Within two and a half years we were debt free, and we haven't looked back since.

I hope this book will help you on your own journey toward financial freedom and that you too will "never look back" as you work toward a checkbook that is at least as buff as the rest of you.

section one:
THINKING THIN

CHAPTER ONE

The Debt Diet

Do You Have a Mild, Moderate,
or Mongo Weight Problem?

When I was in the eighth grade I was five foot eight and weighed 125 pounds. I was a petite size 8. Life was a lot easier when my problems were smaller than my waistline. I was simply too young to appreciate how good I had it. It only took five pregnancies and twenty years for me to fully appreciate my eighth-grade size!

During that time my friend Donna (who was also petite) and I convinced ourselves that we really needed to lose five pounds. Thankfully, my Spanish mom had a no-nonsense approach to life that helped me get a grip before I could even think of falling into the teen trap of a perfect body and eating disorders.

It all started when Donna and I made ourselves "accountable" to each other to only eat nutritional foods and forgo sweets. But my "mamacita" had a plan. She whipped up my favorite chocolate cake, knowing full well that I couldn't resist the sweet indulgence. Later that day my mom drove Donna and me to the mall and, much to my horror, proceeded to tell Donna, in her heavy Spanish accent, about my misdeed:

"Today, Doo-na, Ellie, she no so good."

Donna was polite: "What did Ellie do that wasn't good, Mrs. Rawleigh?"

"Today, Ellie, she eat de cho-co-laa-te cake. She shee-it on her diet!"

I was mortified for more reasons than one. For starters, I wasn't too keen on Donna knowing about my dietary indiscretions. But even worse was the embarrassment I suffered over my mother's pronunciation of *cheat*. It came out of her mouth as a combination of *sheet* and a well-known four-letter word of similar sound.

Later that day I pulled my mom aside. "Mom, can I talk to you a moment?"

My mom stopped dusting the coffee table and gave me her full attention. "Chure, what do chew want to talk about?"

I didn't quite know how to broach the topic, so I just blurted it out: "Well, Mom, it's about your accent."

"What ax-cent? When I *first* come to de United States of Amereeka, I haff an ax-cent. But I no have no ax-cent no more!"

Despite her denial, I was a teenager on a mission and trudged on: "I know, Mom, you've really lost a lot of your accent. But there are still some words that you don't pronounce correctly. And when I'm around my friends the way you say certain words embarrasses me!"

Mom was genuinely concerned: "Well, I no embarrass you for no-thing! You tell me de words and I will practice dem!"

I looked at her eyeball to eyeball. "Mom, earlier today you told my friend Donna that I cheated on my diet. The way you say the word *cheat* sounds like a dirty word!"

The rest of the day as she cleaned house, she "practiced" her enunciation skills.

Each time she dusted the lampshade, cleaned the bathroom mirror, or wiped down a kitchen counter, I overheard her saying, "My daughter, she *shee-it* on her diet."

$ $ $

Whether you're talking about diets or debt, cheating in any language can get you into trouble. And when it comes to finances, many Americans have been toting around sizeable debt and need to go on a "debt diet"—and stick to it!

Stepping on the Scales—How to Know If You're Financially Overweight

You may not know if you really have a debt problem, yet you may have thought, "Hey, I've put on a few dollars here and there." But there's no more effective way to see if you have a problem than to step on the scale. Here are some indicators that you need to go on a debt diet.

- Using credit card cash advances to pay for living expenses
- Using and depending on overtime to meet the month's expenses
- A steadily increasing revolving balance on credit cards
- Using credit to buy things that you used to pay for in cash, such as groceries, gasoline, and clothing (that you do not pay off when the card bill arrives)

- Using an overdraft protection plan on your checking account to pay monthly bills
- Using savings to pay bills
- Using one credit card to pay another
- "Floating" the bills: delaying one bill in order to pay another overdue bill
- Using another loan or an extension on a loan to service your debt
- Using a co-signature on a note
- Paying only the minimum amount due on charge accounts
- A FICO (Fair Isaac Corporation®) score of less than 500 (This is the credit score that lenders often use to evaluate creditworthiness; see the chapter on FICOs later in the book.)

If some or all of these statements describe you, you have a financial weight problem. Your debt load is too heavy. Your belt—your checking balance—is too tight. The devices above may temporarily cover up the weight gain, but they will only worsen the problem in time.

Just like the woman who uses a girdle to "shift the weight around" in an attempt to look thinner, poor money managers have their own "weight shifting" devices to make their debt load appear lighter than it really is.

The following "workout" lists the top ten ways people shift the burden of their debt to try to make it appear less than it really is.

FISCAL FITNESS WORKOUT

TOP TEN "MONEY MOVES" QUIZ

Consider the following ten statements in light of your own attitudes or actions. Rate each with *agree, maybe,* or *disagree.*

1. "I have a large mortgage because all mortgage debt is good debt."
2. "I'll just use a home equity loan to pay off credit card debt."
3. "I'll put it on my credit card."
4. "I need to drive a really nice/new car; it will save on maintenance."
5. "We always get a big tax refund."
6. "I'm going to borrow from my 401(k)/IRA. I'll look into the details later."
7. "I'm not building my 401(k) in this kind of market."
8. "I like/invest in this company because I know them."
9. "I don't want to contribute to a nondeductible IRA because there's no tax benefit."
10. "I should probably refinance, but it really seems like a hassle."

ANSWERS: TOP TEN "MONEY MOVES" QUIZ

1. "I have a large mortgage because all mortgage debt is good debt." *Disagree.* One major reason for debt gain has to do with the "good news/bad news" of recent mortgage rates.

According to Economy.com, the annual household liability has grown 24% since the start of 2003—which is ten percentage points *more* than during the 1991 recession. Part of the increase can be attributed to the increased number of homeowners today—which we all know is "good" debt. It's kind of like the dietary equivalent to having muscle weight instead of fat weight. However, when it comes to finances, at some point the good debt/bad debt logic is going to break down.

For example, the mortgages that many homeowners have today are much larger than they might have had in the past due to lower interest rates. Furthermore, many homeowners have taken advantage of rising home values to use some of their equity to pay off consumer debt such as cars and credit cards.

On one hand, "People have improved their balance sheet because the mix (of debt) is better," said Brian Nottage, Economy.com's director of macroeconomics. "If people are going to rack up debt, better that it's mortgage debt" (Jeanne Sahadi, *CNN/Money* senior writer, Money.cnn.com, Oct. 7, 2003).

The interest rates on HELOCs (home equity lines of credit) tend to be much lower than credit card interest rates, and the interest is usually tax-deductible. Since the risk of not paying your mortgage means a possible foreclosure, the incentive to pay those debts is greater. But what happens when the rates follow the norm of adjusting upward? If you also have a mortgage rate that is adjustable, it means you could suddenly see your debt load rise significantly, and that means more debt weight than ever before.

If home prices slow down or the companies downsize and individuals lose their jobs, debt-laden consumers could find themselves clamoring to work off their debt load in order to fit into the "size 8 jeans" of that lovely new home or car.

2. "I'll just use a home equity loan to pay off credit card debt." *Disagree.* I alluded to this in the previous paragraph, but why, specifically, is this a dumb money move? Lenders love to tout the benefits of using Peter to pay Paul. And when home equity rates are down, it seems like a good move, right? Wrong. According to the Federal Reserve, last year we borrowed $701.5 billion from our home equities, which is up $416.2 billion from 1997. The only way this truly helps is if you completely stop using credit cards to run up those debts—an act of discipline that the average American simply will not do. Therefore, unless you're well above average, it's not a good move. Your debt hole is getting deeper and you don't even realize it because you're able to keep making your mortgage payment and don't see the bottom line of your total debt load.

You want proof? According to Moneycentral.com writer Liz Pulliam Weston (Jan. 28, 2004), "Nearly two-thirds of the people who borrowed against their home equity between 1996 and 1998 to pay off credit cards had run up more card debt within two years, according to a study by Atlanta research firm Britain Associates."

This slowly whittles away the equity you have in your home for use in case of an emergency, such as unemployment, medical expenses, or other financial setbacks.

3. "I'll put it on my credit card." *Disagree.* If your credit card works out more than you do, you likely have a debt weight problem. For example, some consumers feel that by using their credit cards for daily purchases they're building airline miles or they have an interest-free loan until the bill comes due. But buying on credit makes it far easier to overspend. Paying cash is a more conscientious decision, no matter how you look at it. The average person is less likely to buy whenever the urge hits if they're constantly forking over twenty dollar bills to pay for purchases. Plus, fees are becoming more and more prevalent (see chapter 4 for ways you're paying more than ever on credit card fees and penalties).

There are two kinds of debt: good debt vs. bad debt. A mortgage is an example of "good" debt, but consumer debt is the bad kind of debt. Your credit card debt may either be in the card or in the mortgage (on a home equity loan)—but the debt is still there, waiting to be erased.

According to CardWeb.com, at the end of 2002, the average family's debt load was $8,940. That's expensive weight to carry around, making the family more at risk for an average of 16.2% APR for most cards. The amazing fact is that the average family has not only one card but sixteen! That typically includes six bank cards, eight retail cards, and two or three debit cards.

If your credit card works out more than you do, you likely have a debt weight problem.

4. **"I need to drive a really nice/new car; it will save on maintenance."** *Disagree.* We are in love with cars. The American fantasy includes a big house, nice cars, and dream vacations. While we might get good interest rates on our home and econ-

omize on vacations, it's usually the car craze that loads us down with debt in the end. Auto sales have been at near historical levels in the past five years, and the average consumer has paid more than ever for the privilege of owning a cool car.

According to the Consumer Bankers Association, the average new vehicle loan has increased 5% to $21,779 in 2002. The average used vehicle loan rose 12% to $16,542. The trend toward longer loans means that the average consumer will have a car that will not be paid for in less than 49 months. By the time you trade in the car for a new one, the old car is often worth less than the remaining loan value. Buying a new car every five years, as most Americans do, while still owing on the old one, continues to add debt upon debt.

Is it only car and mortgage debt that is weighing us down? Unfortunately, no. We have smart people making dumb money moves that keep them from paying off debt, even when they have the means to do so.

5. **"We always get a big tax refund."** *Disagree.* The operative word here is *big*, meaning more than $2,000 or so. If you are getting this much back in a refund, then you are likely over-withholding on your taxes. Some people just like getting that check every year so they can spend it on vacations, luxury items, or paying off an item they bought in anticipation of the refund. Most tax professionals are exasperated with clients who are getting upward of $10,000 in refunds and are happy about it. It's usually best to adjust the W–4 to have less withheld than to have the "forced savings" of a refund. That way, your money makes money throughout the year instead of sitting stagnant, waiting for you to get it back in the form of a refund.

It's wiser to adjust the W–4 to the correct amount and then use that available income to create a direct deposit into a savings plan. You really can trust yourself to save more and let your money make you money throughout the year—not just at tax time.

6. "I'm going to borrow from my 401(k)/IRA. I'll look into the details later." *Disagree.* The younger the family, the more likely they are to make a dumb money move without knowing the details (penalties, restrictions, and limitations involved) of their financial decision. Let's say a family takes $50,000 in early distributions (withdrawals, not loans) from a 401(k) and IRA to buy a home because they thought they could do so without penalty. Without knowing the "details," they don't realize they are wrong in their assumption. You can only take a $10,000 distribution from your IRA without penalty if you're a *first-time home buyer* and even then you'll *still owe income tax.*

I'm amazed at how many long-term decisions are made as a result of getting casual (and bad) information over a water-cooler conversation! One young family man believed he would only pay a 10% penalty for anything he withdrew over $10,000 from his 401(k) in order to buy a home. Instead, he ended up owing taxes and penalties on the whole amount. It's important to check with your tax professional (hire one, please) before you make major financial decisions. The end result in the case of this young man is that the family got tagged with a $19,000 tax bill because they didn't check the rules and run the numbers.

7. "I'm not building my 401(k) in this kind of market." *Disagree.* Don't deprive yourself of a tax-deferred savings plan for the future because the market is down today. Furthermore, you shouldn't deprive yourself of free money if your employer is matching the contributions! Even if the market is down, you don't have to invest your 401(k) in stocks. You could put your money in a low-risk bond or money market fund until the market bounces back.

8. "I like/invest in this company because I know them." *Disagree.* Suppose a doctor is fond of investing in a particular pharmaceutical company because he is familiar with their products and services. Is that a good reason to buy their stock? No. Similarly, employees tend to own too much company stock because they're overconfident they'll know when to sell. They feel they'll see the writing on the wall internally. I'll sum up that faulty logic in one word: *Enron.*

The best advice is still never to invest more than 10% of your portfolio in any one stock and never more than 30% in a particular sector. Even if the company is owned by your mother!

9. "I don't want to contribute to a nondeductible IRA because there's no tax benefit." *Disagree.* The individual ends up not investing in *any kind* of IRA at all, and the future will not fund itself. The money you put into an IRA might not be tax-deductible, but the interest that grows from that fund is still tax-deferred. This means the money can grow faster than it might in one of the taxable accounts, where you'll pay taxes every year on dividends, capital gains, and interest to Uncle Sam and to your home state.

10. "I should probably refinance, but it really seems like a hassle." *Disagree.* The only reason you should not refinance isn't because of the hassle, but because of the bottom line. If you crunch the numbers on the amount of time it takes to shop for a loan, fill out the paper work, and project the overall benefit, you'll find it truly could be worth "the hassle." For example, if you can save $3,600 per year with a refi, and the process takes about ten hours, you are making around $360 an hour! This is guaranteed income (and tax-free, I might add) and usually worth the time. Just make sure the numbers add up to your advantage in order to make this a smart money move for you.

Assessing Your Debt Diet Needs

Give yourself one point for each question you answered "agree," two points for each "maybe," and three points for each "disagree."

FINANCIALLY FIT:

If you scored between 26 and 30, you weren't swayed by any of the gimmicks or tricks found in the suggested money moves, and you are financially fit (not to mention *smart*).

MILD PROBLEM:

If you scored between 22 and 26, you have a mild debt problem and may want to lose a few pounds to be at top form.

MODERATE PROBLEM:

If your score was between 18 and 22, you are susceptible to making some dumb money moves that could keep you in debt for most of your life. You most likely live above your means and have a mounting debt problem. It would be wise to develop a better understanding of debt and begin a path toward the right attitudes and actions that will help you improve your financial status. Savvy?

Mongo Problem:

If you scored less than 18, you clearly have a significant debt problem that will weigh you down and keep you from reaching the finish line of your financial goals. You need to take deliberate, disciplined action to overcome the problem. If you continue down the path you are currently on, you will likely end up in need of the financial equivalent of a gastric bypass: That is bankruptcy and/or no retirement funds or a financial legacy to pass on to your children. But even in your case, there is still hope for your future.

This test is not scientific and it can be subjective. Therefore, please feel free to retest in light of the information found in the answer portion of this chapter. What you want to identify are attitudes and actions that reveal weak areas that require attention—in other words, the necessity of going on a debt diet. Whether you need to lose a few pounds of debt, or a truckload, the good news is that you are reading this book. So take heart! This could very well be the time when you understand where you are, how you got there, and how you can regain your financial health.

CHAPTER TWO

A Long Line of Big Spenders
Why Do You Do That Thing You Do?

My kids come from a long line of hams.

Our two older daughters have performed in the theater from Los Angeles to New York City, and even on a cruise line. They really brought down the house at their father's Air Force retirement ceremony with their original a cappella arrangement of "The Star-Spangled Banner."

My husband, Bob, played the lead role in the community production of *Scrooge* and never quite got over it. Daniel, Philip, and Bethany never met a role they didn't like, and even our "Sweetpea," Jonathan, played such a pathetic Tiny Tim that members of the audience could be heard crying. The poor baby of the family, Joshua, feels the need to crank up the action even further in an attempt to stand out in a family of drama kings and queens.

Several years ago Tom Hanks produced a movie called *That Thing You Do!* It featured a fictitious "one-hit wonder" band from the '60s that had its fifteen minutes of fame and then broke up. Our family particularly enjoyed the music from the movie. My kids even learned the songs by heart—but Joshua took it to the next level, even at the age of three.

Just last week we pulled out an old family video and watched the then toddler, Joshua, pull out a hairbrush microphone and sing with great passion:

"You, doing dat thing you do
breakin' my heart into a million pieces
wike you always do
and you don't mean to be cruel
you never even knew
about de heartache I been goin' through."

Joshua mustered up such feeling in the grand finale that he got down on his knees, grabbed his heart, and wailed:

"Well, I twy and twy to forget you, girl
but it's just so hard to do
every time you do dat thing you do."

We howled with laughter and all agreed that Joshua was definitely hanging out in the right family tree—the one with hams on its branches instead of leaves.

It's very hard trying to break the mold when you come from a "long line of _____ (you fill in the blank)." Bob came from a long line of big spenders that clashed with my line of big savers. Whatever your case may be, it's easy to use that "long line" line as an excuse to avoid changing. Sure, maybe everyone in your family has always been overweight, had a hot temper, or been eccentric or stingy or whatever. It doesn't mean you have to follow in the familial footsteps—especially if the behavior is destructive.

You may have come from a line of born spenders who had money problems. Maybe no one ever talked about finances in your family, but you can start by opening the lines of communication with your mate and children. Perhaps no one in your family ever went to college. Well, your kids could be the new trendsetters. While it may be true that "you can pick your friends and pick your vegetables, but you can't pick your family"—you can certainly pick a different path for your future. And a journey that leads to the high road when it comes to your family finances will prove well worth the effort it takes to get there.

One of the most constructive things you can do to foster change is to gain an understanding of the financial, emotional, and personal habits that shape your view of finances. Once you realize why you "do that thing you do," then you can make the choices necessary to avoid making the same mistakes that perhaps your parents (and their parents) made. Of course, not everyone reading this book had parents or grandparents who were poor money managers. For those who had *good* financial role models, thank God for such a distinction. But for those of you who didn't and for those who have financial difficulties of your own design, the really good news is that you can change the patterns for your kids—so they'll have a healthy financial legacy to carry on.

Money Personalities

According to Dr. Kathleen Gurney, CEO of Financial Psychology Corporation, and author of *Your Money Personality: What It Is and How You Can Profit From It*, there are nine different money personalities. She wrote, "For most of us, money and our feelings toward it are not static but fluid, dynamic and intense. We love money or we hate it, we fear it, or we worship it, or we enjoy it but we certainly never ignore it." In her years of experience with families in financial conflict she came to the conclusion, "Most of us fail to realize the extent to which our financial personality impacts our financial habits and affects the degree of satisfaction we get from what money we have. There is an inseparable link between our unconscious feelings about money and the way in which we earn, spend, save and invest it" (*www.kathleengurney.com*. Used with permission).

> *"There is an inseparable link between our unconscious feelings about money and the way in which we earn, spend, save and invest it."*

Here's a brief summary of Dr. Gurney's nine money personalities:

ACHIEVERS

These are the second-highest income earners, who are usually college graduates, and most are married. They feel that work, diligence, and effort will pay off better than anything else. They are proud of their accomplishments, but tend to distrust others' honesty with money. They are usually conservative and not interested in risking assets they have worked hard to accumulate. Protection is a primary consideration. These are usually take-charge types, who have a strong need to control their money.

ENTREPRENEURS

This is the most male-dominated profile, driven by a passion for excellence and commitment, which helps them achieve their goals. Despite being the highest income earners, they are workaholics who are not motivated by money alone; it is simply a tool to measure their success. They enjoy the power and prestige money brings and are proud and reward themselves with luxury items. Investing in the stock market is one of their favorite pastimes.

HIGH ROLLERS

These are the thrill seekers who enjoy the ride of financial risk but are only mildly interested in where it takes them. They seek the power and recognition that money brings them. They are creative, extroverted, and competitive. They work hard and play hard, and for them, money is an emotional release. They prefer to risk their assets rather than sit back and be bored by financial security. If they do not learn how to manage their style, they can end up with poor self-esteem and a nagging sense of discontent.

HUNTERS

These personalities are often women and average to above-average income earners who make purchasing decisions with their hearts and not their heads. They are usually highly educated and have a "live for today" financial style. They use impulsive spending as a way to reward themselves. They have a strong work ethic, like the entrepreneurs, but lack the same confidence.

They attribute success to chance rather than ability and judgment. Once they understand their traits, they can make dramatic financial progress and rise above their weaknesses.

MONEY MASTERS

These personalities balance their finances with the degree of contentment and security they derive from their money. They are the No. 1 wealth accumulators even though they don't necessarily earn the most. They rank first in degree of desired involvement with their money and enjoy participation. They trust the recommendations of others and act on sound advice. They do not leave life to chance. Success through determination is their philosophy.

PERFECTIONISTS

They are so afraid of making a mistake that they often avoid making a decision. They forever try harder, but lack self-esteem, especially about their money. They have the least pride in handling financial matters. They have tunnel vision, consider every angle, and find fault with the potential of practically any investment. They are almost impossible to please when it comes to finding suitable investments.

PRODUCERS

They rank high in work ethic, but lower in earned income due to lack of self-confidence in money management skills. This leads to some real frustrations. They work hard, desire more, and feel they have difficulty getting ahead financially. Financial investment/education can be very rewarding since they often don't understand how the money system works. They do not evaluate risks carefully and rarely profit from them.

OPTIMISTS

These are the people to whom money has brought peace of mind. They have the fewest anxieties and tend to be proud and content. They are the least reflective, and their money decisions are somewhat impulsive but not risk oriented. Often in or near retirement, they are more interested in enjoying their money than making it grow. They are not highly involved with their money, taxes, or investments, which could cause them stress and detract from their enjoyment.

SAFETY PLAYERS

They score the lowest in self-determination. They are average earners, and most of their money goes into safe and secure investments. Though they are well educated, they lack the confidence and motivation to reap more growth by taking more calculated risks. They take the path of least resistance and feel they are doing just fine. They tend to repeat the same investment strategies that have worked for them in the past.

As with any other assessment, you are likely going to find that you are a combination of personalities. Some of the traits are assets and others are clearly liabilities, but we can make the best use of our money when we are aware of our basic tendencies and how we can use those as strengths while shoring up the weak areas. For a more complete assessment, you can go to the

Financial Psychology Corporation Web site at *www. kathleengurney.com.*

Money Styles

So what is the difference between a money personality and a money style? The former is who you are and why you tend to view money (and the concept of work) the way you do. The latter, which we're going to discuss in detail, shows how you act. The personality is an inward trait (ideologically), while the style is an outward manifestation (practicality).

According to Gayle Rose Martinez, A.F.E., a mental-health and financial counselor and the author of *Money: A Woman's Perspective* (Rose Petal Press, 2000 *moneyandme.com*), there are several key money styles that people possess. With the exception of the "balancer," each style has its own strengths and weaknesses.

THE SAVER

People with this money style tend to equate money with personal security. They are reluctant to spend money at all or to take investment risks. With a saver, everything is about security, and spending money can make them nervous.

(I've often said I'm a born saver, and my family would agree! I was born on December 28—six weeks early—just in time to get my dad another income tax deduction!)

Strengths: They find the greatest bargains, know how to enjoy themselves without spending money, and love the simple pleasure of getting more for less. They tend to live simply, and they avoid the undue stress that comes with the clutter of massive amounts of consumer goods.

Weaknesses: They tend to miss out on opportunities to enjoy themselves or make investments that could help secure their financial future. They may even have trouble using money for their health or well-being. They can also be judgmental of how others spend their money.

Balance: People with this money style need to apply the following phrase to their view of money: "I will buy things that will help me and my family, and I will not feel guilty about spending money in this way."

The Avoider

This style won't talk about money for anything. They think that if they avoid their financial problems, they will go away. They often feel this way because they do not feel adequate in the area of managing money or they feel guilty about having money to manage. These people have a checkbook but don't write numbers in it; they don't know what anything costs. They don't know what their spouse spends money on, and they will let their spouse handle the money in the family.

Strengths: Since they don't waste time thinking about money, they have more time for other pursuits. They've learned that there is more to life than money and can place a high value on things money can't buy, such as friendships and community.

Weaknesses: They are more likely to be blindsided by financial disaster. I once counseled a neighbor woman who was married to an avoider. What made matters worse was that she was an overspender. She accumulated $45K into consumer debt before he knew anything about it.

Avoiders probably haven't started a retirement account, their credit rating is likely to be in danger, and they are more likely to pay late fees and get hits on their credit report for delinquent or late payments.

Balance: They can begin by taking small steps toward financial understanding. Instead of balancing the checkbook, they can start by entering check numbers and amounts. They can also highlight what they do right because they often believe they can't do anything right.

THE OVERSPENDER

These are people who spend too much due to their inflated view of image. They are also those who seek to constantly pleasure themselves by what money can buy. The image-conscious spenders are free with their dough, making others feel as if they can't keep up with the class and quality the overspender projects. These pleasure-seekers are only happy when they are spending money on something they can enjoy.

Strengths: Because they are risk takers, they are more willing to take a chance investing in a start-up business that could succeed. They have an eye for quality and beauty and can create beautiful homes and wardrobes—even on a budget (if they should ever decide to start one).

Weaknesses: They are impulsive, more likely to have credit card and debt problems, tend to live beyond their means, and have difficulty building a secure foundation for the future. The need for instant gratification makes them think in the short term, and they may not do their homework on goods and services they buy.

Balance: The best thing an overspender can do is create a budget and attempt to live on it. They also need to learn delayed gratification in order to slow down the purchasing process.

The User

These are the power people who see money as a means of controlling their environment or other people. They are aggressive with money, both in spending it and investing it. They often forget that money can be used in ways that hurt other people and can even end up hurting themselves without realizing it.

Strengths: They understand the positive impact of money, even though they don't always choose to concentrate on that element. They can use money to promote social good and improve their community. If they are willing to adjust their money habits, they can have a tremendously positive impact on their world.

Weaknesses: They can use money to the harm of their environment and families. They think power comes from money and can feel powerless if they somehow lose money due to a job layoff or unforeseen circumstances.

Balance: Users could develop a budget that emphasizes time instead of money. Such a budget may help them devote more time to less money-oriented pursuits, such as visiting with the family, playing games, or reading a good book.

THE BALANCER

This is a person whose attitude toward the use of money best reflects who he or she is—the understanding that money is basically a tool. Martinez says this personality "remembers that there is more to life than money and keeps her financial life balanced with other aspects of her life."

As you go back through this chapter, take a few notes. Write down the characteristics of your money *personality* as well as your money *style*. Write the strengths and weaknesses of each. Decide what steps you can take to bring your personality and style into balance. Do the same thing for your spouse and then determine how different styles and personalities may have caused conflict in the past and what you can do to minimize financial conflict in the future.

FISCAL FITNESS WORKOUT

"ARE YOU BETTER OR WORSE OFF THAN YOUR PARENTS?"

Yes, most money personalities tend to follow in the footsteps of the "long line" of the ancestors that preceded them. I'm sure there are quite a few people reading this book who have a family "line" to overcome, whether emotionally, spiritually, or financially. Our family of origin can impact us both negatively and positively, but how does this add up in our lives today? Are we better or worse off than our parents were financially? How do the bottom lines from two generations compare?

Here's an interesting chart[1] from Warren and Tyagi's *Two-Income Trap* (Basic Books, 2004), based on analysis of a consumer expenditure survey. How do your finances compare?

	1973 Family (one breadwinner)		Today's Family (two breadwinners)	
Income	$38,700		$67,800	
	Expense	% of Income	Expense	% of Income
Mortgage	$5,310	13%	$9,000	13%
Insurance	$1,030	3%	$1,650	2%
Taxes[2]	$9,288	24%	$22,374	33%
Car(s)[3]	$5,140 One car	13%	$8,200 Two cars	12%
Preschool/Day Care	N/A		$9,670	14%
Income Left Over	$17,834	46%	$17,045	25%

According to Elizabeth Warren and Amelia Warren Tyagi, coauthors of *The Two-Income Trap: Why Middle-Class Mothers and Fathers Are Going Broke,* the average two-income middle-class family today earns 75% more than the typical single-income family did thirty years ago. But today's family, they say, ends up with less money for everyday living expenses and savings.

---

[1] All figures are annual and inflation-adjusted to dollars in the year 2000. Each family owns a 3-BR home and has two kids: a toddler and a grade-schooler in public school. Today's family has two cars, since both parents work.
[2] Includes income taxes and property taxes.
[3] Includes payments, maintenance, and gas.

"Why? The costs of housing and a good education are killing them" (Jeanne Sahadi, *CNN/Money* senior writer).

It's amazing to think that one of the primary reasons we are not better off financially than our parents were is because of the price of education. But take the scenario of a liberal arts major now teaching school. She marries a man who is also a teacher, and both have maxed-out student loans to pay back. This particular couple is locked into working full time for the majority of their children's formative years. With little room for advancement or the opportunity to earn substantially more in today's world, the male head of the household often cannot provide for his family without his wife's help.

If they didn't have so much student loan debt, it would be a different story. So the bottom line is that you do not want to borrow on your own future—or your children's—to pay for today's education. If you do, your children might have to spend the majority of their formative years in day care, absent from both parents. (See chapter 11, "College Crunches.")

The good news is this: If you understand your money personality and follow the advice found in the rest of this book, you can lose the debt weight, be an ongoing source of encouragement to others, and be the kind of success model your children will want to emulate. The choice is yours.

CHAPTER THREE

I Would Be Happy If . . . I Were Rich and Thin

Our Attitude About Money

Most people like the color green.

It makes them feel as if they're in high clover.

Have you ever watched kids with a cardboard box go "sledding" in the summer on a clover-covered hill? Maybe you remember those childhood days yourself. If you waxed the bottom of the box, and the hill was steep enough, you could gain momentum and have a high-flying ride.

Green can be a good color for most folks. We need to have enough of the green stuff in order to conquer the hill of life, have fun, and enjoy the ride. Money can be a four-leaf clover when it accomplishes what we want it to, but the lack of it can paint our world shades of gray or even black.

Our attitude toward money helps to define our relationship with it—whether we have a healthy perspective on money or whether money becomes a force that controls our life in a negative way. See what money attitudes you can discover from the famous people in the following money/wealth quotes:

Said of money: "I don't necessarily like it, but it quiets my nerves."

—Joe Lewis

When asked, "How much is enough money?" the billionaire didn't hesitate and replied, "Always just a little more."

—J. Paul Getty

Money never made a man happy yet, nor will it. There is nothing in its nature to produce happiness. The more a man has, the more he wants. Instead of its filling a vacuum, it makes one.

—Benjamin Franklin

Happiness is not based on money, and the best proof of that is our family.

—Christina Onassis

Do your givin' while you're livin', then you're knowin' where it's goin'.

—Chuck Swindoll (*Tale of a Tardy Oxcart*)

The lack of money is the root of all evil, not the love of it.

—George Bernard Shaw

You spend a billion here, you spend a billion there. Sooner or later it adds up to real money.

—Senator Everett Dirkson

The debtor is in servitude to the one who lends to him.

—Larry Burkett (adapted from Proverbs 22:7b)

I'd like to live as a poor man with lots of money.

—Pablo Picasso

Virtue has never been as respectable as money.
> —Mark Twain

The government's view of the economy could be summed up in a few short phrases: If it moves, tax it. If it keeps moving, regulate it. And if it stops moving, subsidize it.
> —Ronald Reagan

A wealthy man is one who earns $100 a year more than his wife's sister's husband.
> —H. L. Mencken

With money in your pocket, you are wise and you are handsome and you sing well too.
> —Yiddish Proverb

If the greenback becomes the center of life, then it becomes a demanding master. Do we worship the green so that it has become a god? Do we have to "wear" our green so others can see it and thereby define success by what we drive, own, and wear? Speaking of "wearing o' the green," my husband and I were recently in Ireland and stayed at a number of bed and breakfasts. At one gorgeous three-hundred-year-old home, we were having tea by firelight. The retired homeowner, Marc, said, "Aye, the probl'm, with ye Americans is dat ya spend all yer time a makin' the money, spendin' the money, or savin' the money. What ya ferget is how to enjoy life. Aye . . . ya have to slow down, lassie, and be a thinkin' on livin' a bit."

Aye.

The Irishman had it right. Many Americans dream of the day they will be able to take a dream vacation, buy a dream home, or obtain that dream car. It seems too that the definition of *perfect* or *enough* seems to change with the years.

For example, back in 1941 the average size for a woman was thought to be size 8, and many thought that was perfect. But the average got bumped up to size 12 in recent years, and the most current report by Size USA, a survey sponsored by clothing and textile companies, says that the average size is now 14. While the average has increased, the ideal has shrunk, with women striving to fit into sizes 2, 1, and even 0! Our ideas for financial perfection have also changed with the times. The American definition of *rich* has over the years shifted as well (*Sizing Up America: Signs of Expansion* by Kate Zernike, *New York Times*, March 1, 2004).

When asked what defines *rich,* a lot of people say it means never having to worry about money again and working only if the mood strikes (Jeanne Sahadi, *CNN/Money*, July 2003). It's a definition that could work, couldn't it? Let's look at what it takes to be "rich" by these standards. One financial planner, Blanche Lark Christerson, Director of the Wealth Planning Strategies Group at Deutsche Bank, figures that for married couples with two young children and a lifestyle of spending $375,000 per year, they would be set for life (with or without a job) if they had at least $15 million. This presumes they would preserve capital and want to leave their heirs an inheritance. The same expert says that if these lucky people are single, then they could get by on a mere $10 million.

Jon Duncan, a certified financial planner, has a different estimate. He says that if you are in your early forties, are married and have kids, will live to be age ninety, and if you don't spend more than $200,000 per year, you could live on $7.5 million. If you spent $150,000 a year, you could get by on $5 million, and if you live on the bare bones of $100,000 per year, you would still need $2.5 million. These estimates, says Duncan, will not allow you to leave your heirs anything at all.

Do these numbers surprise you? It's not about the numbers, it's about attitude. According to Spectrum Group, a consulting firm specializing in affluent markets, only about 0.45% of households have a net worth of $5 million or more, excluding primary residences. I think most of the people reading this book would think that anyone who lives on $5 million, or even $1 million, is "rich."

Some people have the attitude that the guy in their circle of friends who has more than they do is "rich." Others who make six figures a year don't consider themselves "rich" because they don't have millions in a cash reserve. Obviously, a million bucks just ain't what it used to be.

Jeanne Sahadi (*CNN/Money*) says, "There's another reason I'd argue you can't pin a number on 'rich.' Rich isn't just a quantitative experience. It's a qualitative one. Money is great, but only if it contributes to your sense of well-being rather than detracts from it."

It seems that if you continue to try to keep up with the neighbors by buying your way into a successful state of mind, you will never have enough—no matter how much you own or make. On the other hand, you could suddenly find yourself a wealthy person and not find the satisfaction you always thought wealth would bring.

There's a fascinating group I'd love to be a part of called "Money, Meaning, and Choices" (*www.mmcinstitute.com*). This group works with people who have made or acquired sudden wealth. One of their clients, John, a forty-three-year-old software designer, said:

> Having money has turned out to be more emotionally complicated than I ever could have imagined. . . . I feel uncomfortable with some of the comments and reactions I am getting from people. . . . I'm reasonably content with my marriage and work but something is missing . . . now that I have the time to look at how I spend my day, I'm no longer sure of how to balance my priorities. . . . I'm wondering what really is important to me.

There are three basic reasons why people who "make it" in terms of monetary or material success do not find fulfillment in the wealth itself:

1. *Emotional Satisfaction*—Money doesn't emotionally satisfy a human being. The MMC Institute works with people who have achieved this success and found that the "suddenly rich" have no place to explore matters of money and meaning. In fact, many of these topics suddenly become taboo among friends and family of the nouveau riche. A typical response would be, "Oh, I should have *your* problems." This new status and the emotions that accompany sudden wealth often distance them from those who matter most.

2. *Personal Priorities*—It's easy to get priorities out of balance. No matter how much we earn, we need to find creative ways of developing a lifestyle that is closely aligned with our core values and interests. Whether we're rich or poor, we have to set boundaries in the areas of relationships, work, and community.

3. *Purpose*—A final area where riches will never satisfy is the area of finding purpose in life. All human
beings long to discover spheres of interest that add meaning and passion to our lives. We'd like to believe we are
here for a specific purpose beyond that of simply accumulating wealth.

Some people achieve it all and yet discover that riches don't
satisfy. Others seem to have very little, yet have learned to be
content. I think George Bernard Shaw put it well when he
wrote his opening words to the play *Man and Superman:*

This is the true joy in life, the being used for a purpose recognized by yourself as a mighty one; the being
thoroughly worn out before you are thrown on the scrap
heap; the being a force of nature instead of a feverish self-
ish little clod of ailments and grievances complaining that
the world will not devote itself to making you happy.

The healthiest attitude about wealth is to realize that the
happiest people are not those who have suddenly found wealth,
but those who have found purpose. By finding purpose—bringing it out in ourselves and in others and putting it to good use,
we find true wealth—a wealth that stock market downturns or
economic slumps cannot take away. But this is an individual pursuit. No one can decide to make you content in your financial
situation but *you.* You choose to find purpose. You choose to find
contentment. You choose to find joy. Your spouse cannot do it
for you, neither can your preacher or your friend. Mother Teresa
said, "Do not wait for leaders. Do it alone, person to person."
She was referring to the wealth of purpose as demonstrated by
where you put your time, efforts, and wealth.

To read more about people whose lives have had a kind of meaningful, singular purpose, go to *www.powerofpurpose.org*.

The happiest people are not those who have suddenly found wealth, but those who have found purpose.

As this chapter closes, our Fiscal Fitness exercise is to take time for meditation and personal reflection. Ask yourself the following questions.

FISCAL FITNESS WORKOUT

MONEY ATTITUDE QUIZ

- How much money will it take for me to be happy?
- Which of the quotes at the beginning of the chapter best fit my attitude about money, wealth, and purpose?
- If my debts were all paid today, would I be happy?
- If my salary doubled, how would I spend the money? Would a doubled salary be enough to get everything I need or want, or would I need just a little more?
- How is my attitude toward money affecting my relationships?
- How do I see the purpose of money?
- What is my personal purpose in life?
- What are my priorities—do these need to change?
- Does my PalmPilot or calendar reflect the priorities I mentioned in the previous question?

47

- What can I change to bring my priorities, my life, more into balance?

It may seem odd to venture into the philosophical in the middle of a book about debt. But there are reasons you're in debt, and one of the primary reasons has to do with your attitude about money. If you can begin to evaluate and prioritize, then you have the tools to reorganize your financial goals if necessary. You may very well find that money is simply a power tool to fulfill your purpose in life.

The following is a fun, albeit very unscientific, exercise that will help you see how *your* priorities line up:

Priorities Test[1]

There are five things going on simultaneously that need to be taken care of:

1. The telephone is ringing.
2. The baby is crying.
3. Someone is knocking at the front door or ringing the doorbell.
4. There is laundry hanging on the line outside and it begins to rain.
5. The water faucet in the kitchen is running.

In what order do you take care of the problems? Jot down your order. Each represents something in your life. When finished, see next page to find out what your answers represent.

---

[1]From *www.allfunpages.com.*

HERE ARE THE RESULTS OF YOUR TEST

1. The phone represents your job or career.
2. The baby represents your family.
3. The visitor represents your friends.
4. The laundry represents your sex life.
5. The running water represents money or wealth.

How close did this test match your priorities in life?

I realize that sometimes "family finances" do not rank as a high priority because the tyranny of the urgent tends to take precedence. Managing money doesn't even appear on most people's list of "Fun Things I Like to Do." But if we pay adequate attention to where our money goes today, we will have more time to reap the benefits in the future. So remember: Manage your finances today for a fun tomorrow!

CHAPTER FOUR

Beauty and the Beast Revisited

Plastic Problems: Real Solutions

You saw the movie.

You saw the play on television.

You may have seen the sing-along.

But nothing compares with seeing *Beauty and the Beast* on Broadway. The costumes and set cost millions, the actors and actresses are the top in their field, the director is relentless in rehearsals, and the producer is a perfectionist. These are all the ingredients for an amazing experience while sitting in the comfort of a red crushed velvet theater seat just off Broadway on 46th Street.

A successful play is one that tells an effective story. This particular play tells the story of a man who was beautiful on the outside, but lacked character. He was transformed into a beast, an experience that made him so bitter that his internal behavior mirrored his outward appearance. He had become beastly through and through.

It took the unconditional love of a beautiful girl to search for and find the beauty of character within the man. When his spirit was touched by this love, it transformed him inside—and out.

Our checkbooks and credit cards can play the role of either

Beauty or the beast in our lives and in the lives of our loved ones. If you had to classify your finances today, which would they resemble more—Beauty, or the beast? If, like the beast, you have little regard for how your spending affects others (your family), if you are centered on the here and now instead of delayed gratification, if you are too busy to be bothered with mundane things like a budget and limits, your finances may very well begin to look like the following chart:

THE BEAST'S (OVER) CHARGE ACCOUNTS*

Year	Amount Overspent	Accumulated Interest	End of Year Balance (Debt)
1	$1,200	$104	$1,304
2	1,200	463	2,863
3	1,200	1,128	4,728
4	1,200	2,157	6,957
5	1,200	3,621	9,621
6	1,200	5,608	12,808
7	1,200	8,217	16,617
8	1,200	11,572	21,172
9	1,200	15,818	26,618
10	1,200	21,129	33,129
11	1,200	27,714	40,914
12	1,200	35,821	50,221
13	1,200	45,749	61,349
14	1,200	57,855	74,655
15	1,200	72,562	90,562
Totals	$18,000	$72,562	$90,562

*Based on spending only $100 over budget each month.

This chart vividly illustrates how a modest amount of accumulating debt can cause finances to self-destruct. This particular beast would, more than likely, have destroyed itself financially well before the fifteen-year point. But the average American family's debt load is far more than $1,200 each year!

Some argue that the airline miles or other "benefits" they earn justify their constant use of credit card(s). But buying on credit makes it far easier to overspend. Industry statistics show that consumers spend more using a credit card than with cash or checks because they are not limited to what they have on hand (*www.key.com*). Paying cash is a more conscientious decision, no matter how you look at it.

Is all credit bad, or can credit be used as a tool? Let's find some answers to these common and important questions.

> *Paying cash is a more conscientious decision, no matter how you look at it.*

The Beast: Credit Card Warning Signs

The following are *some* (but not all) of the indicators that you need to cut down on (or cut up!) the plastic beast (some of these were mentioned earlier, but they bear repeating!):

- A steadily increasing revolving balance on credit cards
- Using credit to buy things that you used to pay for in cash, such as groceries, gasoline, and clothing (and not paying them off when the card bill arrives)
- Using one credit card to pay another
- Paying only the minimum amount due on charge accounts

• Transferring balances to new cards only to run up balances again

How Do Hidden Credit Card Costs Make Me Beastly, and What Are Some Beautiful Solutions?

The credit card industry's competition for customers has never been more fierce, but some credit cards can cost you more now than ever. If you're not careful, you may become prey to legal methods that some credit card companies use to charge you more for using their cards—especially if they feel you are becoming a higher risk. It's not that credit card companies are big, bad, scary people who are out to get you. It's simply because credit card delinquency rates rose 30% not long ago, bankruptcy filings remain near all-time-high levels, and credit card lenders are taking the biggest hit. They have to recoup their losses.

That's why it's important to choose your lender very carefully.

The Beast: Waking the Dead

If you have an old, unpaid credit card lurking in your closet, then beware when you decide to open a new card. According to Liz Pulliam Weston, writer for *MSN Money:*

> John Witters of Davie, Florida, was delighted to get a low-rate offer from Capital One a while back. After all, his credit wasn't the greatest, thanks in part to about $1,500 worth of credit card bills he failed to pay to his previous credit card company. . . . Imagine his surprise

when that $1,500 debt showed up on his new credit card. Witters insists that he didn't know he was "reaffirming" or agreeing to pay the old debt when he signed up for the new card. [The new lender] is equally insistent that the deal was spelled out in the solicitation he received.

Currently some lenders are buying previous debts from other creditors and trying to entice borrowers to repay the debt with a new credit card. This is a legal action as long as these terms are disclosed to the client—but sometimes the information is in the fine print of the document the client signs. Here are some steps you can take to avoid this situation.

FISCAL FITNESS WORKOUT

Tips From a Beauty

PAY OLD DEBTS

The most obvious way to stay a step ahead of a spotty credit history is to make good on old debts. Even if your debt has been written off and there are no creditors breathing down your neck, you could contact the previous creditor and make arrangements to pay down that debt. Not only could it help improve your credit score, an old debt that is settled can no longer come back to haunt you.

READ THE FINE PRINT

Remember that just because a new bank or different credit card company is offering a new card—you could still potentially owe an old debt if the debts have been bought by a new company. If you don't understand the terms, call the potential creditor and ask for clarification before you sign on the bottom line.

The Beast: Statute of Limitations Denied

Not all collection agencies operate within the guidelines of the Fair Credit Reporting Act, which states that a bad debt is dropped off a credit record after the seven-year statute of limitations has been met. Some credit agencies have even been known to purchase the bad debts, report them with new dates, and give new life to old debts for another seven years. This is highly illegal according to the Federal Trade Commission. Here are two steps you can take if you find yourself in this unusual (yet increasingly recurring) situation.

More Fiscal Fitness Tips From Beauty

THOU DOST PROTEST

If you the consumer protest, you can request that the collection agency investigate and correct the illegal entry. This should be your first line of defense.

THE NEXT STEP

If the collection agency refuses to do this, the consumer should contact the National Association of Consumer Advocates (*www.naca.net*) for adequate recourse. At this site, there's a list of possible legal representation from attorneys who specialize in these kinds of disputes.

The Beast: Fee-Fee, the Wonder Dog

This old dog is learning new tricks. The amount of money collected in late fees has risen four times in less than a decade, an increase of almost $6 billion. Yes, believe it or not, lenders collected $7.3 billion worth of fees last year alone.

It's not that there has been a massive outbreak of payment delinquency among consumers; it's just that the penalties have become much, much greater. Here are some facts to consider:

LATE FEES

The average late fee in the summer of 1994 was $11.97. This rose to the current average of $30.04, according to CardTrak. Don't think that just because you have a Platinum card that you'll pay lower fees. According to CardWeb.com:

> While "Platinum" Visa and MasterCards have generally come to signify the issuer's highest credit limits and lowest pricing, a "Platinum" offer may also include some of the highest fees for making a late payment, going over the credit limit, or taking a cash advance. According to a sampling of "Platinum" solicitations, dispatched in June

and captured by CardWeb's new "CardWatch" service, "Platinum" late payment fees are 31% higher than the industry average.

OVER-LIMIT FEE

More bad news, the fee for going over your limit rose in the same period from an average of $12.57 to $28.01.

CASH-ADVANCE FEE

The fee for a cash advance used to be a $2 minimum and $10 maximum with a 2% interest fee. Today they are between $10 and $50 and charging 3% interest. The interest is charged as soon as the clock starts running on those advances. The cash advance interest fee is also more likely to be higher than the interest rate charged on purchases. Those are three reasons you should never use a credit card for a cash advance.

GRACE PERIOD

It is easier to make a late payment than ever before because some lenders have reduced grace periods (the time you have to pay your bill before it is considered late) from thirty days in 1990 to an average grace period of twenty-one days in 2004. Two out of three people paid at least one late fee last year. Also be aware that a credit card company may suddenly change their grace period on a longtime account you've held for many years. For example, they could change it from twenty-five days to only twenty-one days; however, they must give notification of the change before it goes into effect.

CARD FEES

This is the annual fee your lender charges to allow you to keep their card. While the introductory fee may be minimal, or even waived, the subsequent fees could be quite high—even doubled in some cases. It pays to know what you're paying on your annual fee.

Training Fee-Fee the Wonder Dog

You can resist this old dog's new tricks by retraining yourself when it comes to credit card payments and transactions. Here are a few countermeasures:

ACT IMMEDIATELY

When your credit card bill arrives, pay the minimum payment right away—especially if you have a twenty-one-day billing cycle. You can always send a larger payment at the end of the month—and hopefully you will, because it's important to start paying down your debt as soon as possible.

When your credit card bill arrives, pay the minimum payment right away—especially if you have a twenty-one-day billing cycle.

AUTOMATE IT

If you know you are going to be carrying a balance for a while, set up an automated payment with your online banking institution. This payment would be for a few dollars more than your estimated minimum payment each month. This way you can make sure you won't have a late fee.

Ask!

If you are charged a late fee and you do not have a history of late charges or other delinquencies, call the lender and ask them to remove the late fee. Many will do this if you take the time to ask and if you fit the "good customer" criteria.

Avoid Cash

Use your debit card to get cash instead of your credit card. If you get into the habit of getting cash on your credit card, you not only pay additional fees, but you could go into greater debt and have little or nothing to show for it.

Annual Fee Reduction

About two and one half months before your card is set to renew, or if you receive a notice that your old card is being replaced by the same lender with a new and improved card, call the credit card company and ask them what the annual card fee will be. If you are a good customer with a solid history with this company, ask them to waive the annual fee in order to keep you as a happy customer.

Pay Attention

Your creditor is required to notify you of all changes in advance. This includes the change in grace periods, interest rates, and card provider changes. In the fine-print brochure you receive, you are allowed to decline the new terms and pay off your account under the old terms, but you would also have to give up the card and not charge new items.

The Beast: Do You Know Your Credit Card Habits? They Do!

I don't want to get you panicky over the idea that Big Brother is watching you, but—*Big Brother is watching you*! Lenders do track your charges, payment, and spending habits. If you are aware of how this can impact you, then you'll be less likely to pay more in interest and fees. Here are some of the areas you need to be aware of where you are being watched:

New Accounts

Lenders consistently review credit reports. If you are opening too many charge accounts (even for furniture or a 0% APR automobile), you could take a hit with an increased APR on your credit card.

Late Payments

Not only will you pay a substantial late fee, as we just discussed, but you could also pay a higher rate if you are late with as little as two payments.

Revolving Balance

It's important not to charge more than 50% of the available credit on the card. For example, if you have a card with a limit of $8,000, in order to keep the best rates, you should carry no more than $4,000 as a revolving balance on that card.

MAXING OUT CARDS

If you are maxing out your credit limit, it could send a message to lenders that you are getting into debt overload with the potential of not having the means to pay your debts. Consequently, you could get hit with a higher rate because you are becoming a greater risk to the lender.

PAYING THE MINIMUM

In the past lenders seemed to encourage borrowers to carry a balance and to only pay the minimum payment due on the debt. They even reinforced this concept by making the minimum payment only 1% of the total debt instead of the standard 2.5% to 3%. But things have changed in recent years. Those "min" paying customers are beginning to be viewed with suspicion. Can they pay all their debts? Are they paying the minimums because they are living month to month with no additional funds, yet still have available credit? Not only does min paying mean paying tons of interest, it could indicate that you are an "at risk" customer who may be more likely to default on a loan. Some minimum payment customers are now having their rates raised to as much as 20% simply because they do not attempt to pay down the balance. This habit also lowers your FICO scores.

FICO

Your credit rating, or FICO score, affects your rate. If you don't know your credit rating, you can be sure your lender does! Customers with a lower credit rating (generally 600 or less, depending upon the lender) will pay a higher APR. I talk more about FICOs in chapter 6—what they are, why they're important, and what you can do to improve them.

Making Big Brother Into a Good Son

You do not have to be afraid of Big Brother or be at his mercy. Knowledge is power, and now that you are learning what creditors look for in establishing rates and fees, you can make this knowledge work to your advantage. Here are some specific things you can start doing *today* to lower your APR or to make sure it isn't suddenly raised:

PAY ON TIME

Paying your bills on time will help you keep your rates down, and we've already discussed a couple of ways to make sure you pay your bills on time.

PAY MORE

Even if you pay $5 more than your minimum payment, you are *still* technically "paying down" your debt, and this will be reflected on your credit history.

New Applications

Be aware that every store account you open (to get that 15% discount offer), furniture charge account (to get the "twelve months, same as cash" deal), or appliance sales account (who can pass up the free, extended warranty?) will hit you on your credit rating. Keep these applications to a minimum. Or better yet, turn them down as a policy.

Don't Max Out

Don't consistently max your credit card limit unless you can pay it off at the end of the month. Better to divide the debt among a couple of cards than to keep maxing out a single card.

Don't Min Out

Some points are worth reinforcing: Pay more than your minimum for better credit health. If you only pay the minimum on a $2,000 balance, it will take you eighteen years to pay off the debt and you will have paid a total of $4,600 with interest! Whereas if you pay only $25 more than the minimum on a $5,000 balance, it would take sixteen years off the time it takes to pay the debt, PLUS it would save you $3,000 in interest.

Credit Report

You need to check your credit report at least twice a year. If you have free access to the report, courtesy of your lenders, take advantage of the offer. Dispute errors (more on that later), check for fraud (possible identity theft), and close down department store cards that you don't use. Go to *www.freecreditreport.com* for a copy of your report. Or, contact any of the three credit reporting agencies directly at:

> Equifax: (800) 685–1111 or *www.equifax.com*
> Experian: (888) 297–3742 or *www.experian.com*
> TransUnion: (800) 888–4213 or *www.transunion.com*

The Beast: Transfer Trouble

You probably get several offers a month from lenders who will give you a fantastic APR if you transfer your existing debt load to their new card. Have you ever been tempted to take them up on their offer? Or, have you ever *done* it? I've worked with people who have given in to the quick fix once, and before they knew it they were transfer addicts! Here are the traps to be aware of in the "transfer temptation":

BAIT AND SWITCH

Sometimes a lender will make a great initial offer at a fantastic rate in order to get you to transfer your balances to their card. However, unless you have a good credit score—you may not even get the great rate! Even some pre-qualified accounts don't get the lower APR. Instead, you might get approved for the card, but at a higher rate.

FEES

Some consumers don't realize there could be substantial fees for balance transfers. Most lenders charge at least 3% for balance transfers, which could eliminate the benefit of the lower interest rate.

LONGEVITY

Part of the "good" FICO score is determined by how long you've kept a card and been a good customer. The longer you've held a card (and paid well), the greater your credit limit tends to be, and an unused credit balance looks good on your credit rating. If you cancel a card you've had ten years in order to get the lower APR on a new card, you may lose the benefit of longevity with the first credit card company, thereby allowing your credit rating to take a hit.

HIGHER RATES FOR NEWBIES

While you may (or may not) get a great rate on balance transfers, your new purchases might still be subject to the higher rate. In fact, if the new card's primary rates are higher for you, you could end up paying more in the long run on your new charges if you are a regular charging customer. The reason for this is that all the payments you make will first go toward the lower rate charges while the higher rates continue to accumulate interest longer.

FICO HIT

Opening and closing multiple credit card accounts hurts your credit score. The lenders can see what you're doing—trying to float the balance and go for the best rate. In the long run you will likely hurt your credit score and end up paying as much (if not more) in fees and hidden higher interest rates.

Beauty Says: Transfer Help

Credit can be a tremendous tool, and not all transfers are a bad deal for the consumer, but it's important to know how and when to make a transfer. Here are some tips that will help you make the most of these opportunities.

Two for One

If you are going to use a card for balance transfers (and it meets the criteria in this section), use it only for the lower transfer rate and use your old, established card for new purchases. That way you're paying the best interest rate on the transfer balance, and you pay the best (or lower) interest rate on your existing card.

Count the Cost

If you do want to transfer a balance to a new card, get a disclosure, up front, of transfer fee costs and any setup fees for the card itself as well as the annual renewal fee. After you've done your math, then determine if it will be a good value to switch. A great tool to calculate these costs as well as get card descriptions and fees can be found at *www.Bankrate.com*.

Minimize Numbers of Cards

Try to keep your balances on one or two cards in order to keep up with the time constraints on introductory APRs, payment due dates, and other card details. You are more likely to make a mistake (and pay a large penalty fee for your error) while trying to keep up with too many different cards.

READ THE FINE PRINT

Before you apply, make sure the "bait and switch" tactic we described above will not apply to the new card or to your situation. See how long you will qualify for the lower introductory APR (for the lifetime of the balance, or for only a few months) and make your decision accordingly.

The Beast: The Wrong Card Could Add Fat to Your Dream Vacation

Let's take a mental break right now and have a little vacation. We deserve it after delving into the nitty-gritty world of credit card debt. If you were given a free trip anywhere in the world and a credit card to use for a shopping spree, where would you go? Picture yourself on the beaches of Bora Bora, having the spa treatment, or in the Waterford crystal factory in Ireland, selecting that exquisite vase. Maybe you would peruse fashions in France, shop for Lladros in Spain, buy Hummels in Germany, or snarf down chocolates in Switzerland. Can you picture yourself there yet?

Unfortunately, most of us don't have a free shopping spree coming on our credit card when we have the rare opportunity to travel abroad. Not only do most of us have to pay the bill, we also have to pay the fees associated with exchanging foreign money. The exchange rates vary greatly from card to card, and you need to think strategically about which card you take on that dream vacation. Here are some facts that could help you make that decision, and may you one day be blessed with this dilemma, because it means you're on your way!

Paying Abroad

Credit cards tend to be the best way to purchase items overseas—you have less risk of cash being stolen, the cardholder tends to get a better exchange rate, and you don't have to worry about re-exchanging unused money on your trip home. They are also more convenient than traveler's checks, because not all businesses take traveler's checks overseas.

Fees

The typical fee for overseas transactions on your credit card ranges from 1% to 3%, depending upon the card. Sometimes the only way to find out what rate your card charges is by calling the credit card company and asking them. Liz Pulliam Weston, financial writer for *MSN Money*, says:

> You might not have even realized this happened; typically, the fee doesn't even show up on your statement, since it's embedded in the exchange rate you're shown. But it should be revealed somewhere in the fine print of your cardholder agreement, or you can call your issuer and ask (*moneycentral.msn.com*).

It All Adds Up

The difference between 1% and 3% could add up if you plan on bringing back some great bargains. For example, on $3,000 worth of goods, you would pay about $90 less in fees at the lower rate, and every little bit helps.

Flying Happy

So what do you do if you want to get the best rate on overseas credit card charges? It's really quite simple:

- Call your credit card companies to find the best overseas transaction rates.
- Take more than one kind of card. It's not safe to assume that all businesses accept Visa, so bring along an American Express or MasterCard as well. Just make the majority of your purchases on the card with the better rate when you have a choice of cards.

In conclusion, it's important to know how the credit card industry operates and how you can use credit as a tool rather than having it use you. You absolutely can take charge of your credit cards if you act on the new knowledge you now have.

section two:
FISCAL FITNESS

CHAPTER FIVE

The Celebrity Diet

How to Become a Millionaire

Just like a food diet, when it comes to going on a debt diet, we sometimes need to find the motivation to get started. Even after we've taken those first few steps toward becoming financially fit, it's still important to keep making progress—especially if we hit a plateau in our debt loss. I've known friends who have put a photo of a celebrity on their refrigerator to encourage themselves to resist temptation when they get the urge to splurge. Even Yours Truly has a photo of a slender model on her fridge that stands between me and my ice cream.

If we were to choose a celebrity to inspire us to stick to our debt diet, who might that be? Donald Trump? Ted Turner? Tom Cruise? Most likely we would choose someone who is a millionaire, or perhaps a billionaire. They are the ones who have arrived and "made it" when it comes to money. There's a common advantage that most celebrities have when it comes to keeping a beautiful trim body—they hire lots of help! Most hire a trainer, a personal chef, and a makeup artist. They may have their photos airbrushed and multiple plastic surgeries.

You could create millionaire kids with as little as $3K a year invested for five years.

Well, I've got news for you. Millionaires are not always the "rich and famous" we imagine them to be. They aren't always the people with the six-figure incomes. In fact, the average millionaire isn't a celebrity at all—-they're the average Joes who might live next door to you.

Yes, the average millionaire is the head of a hard-working family in mainstream America who has successfully spent less than he made and invested the difference over a significant period of time. In fact, you could create millionaire kids with as little as $3K a year invested for five years. Let's look at our fiscal fitness chart on how to become a millionaire through the miracle of compounding interest.

How to Become a Fiscally Fit Millionaire

	SAVES EARLY		SAVES LATE		SAVES LATER	
AGE	Invests 3K/Year	Value	Invests	Value	Invests	Value
15	$3K	$3,300				
16	3K	6,930				
17	3K	10,923				
18	3K	15,315				
19	3K	20,146	$3K	$3,300		
20		22,161	3K	6,930		
21		24,377	3K	10,923		
22		26,815	3K	15,315		
23		29,496	3K	20,146		
24		32,446	3K	25,461		
25		35,691	3K	31,307		
26		39,260	3K	37,738		
27		43,186		41,512	$3K	$3,300
28		47,505		45,663	3K	6,930
29		52,255		50,229	3K	10,923
30		57,481		55,252	3K	15,315

31	$63,229	$60,778	$3K	$20,146
32	69,552	66,855	3K	25,461
33	76,507	73,541	3K	31,307
34	84,158	80,895	3K	37,738
35	92,574	88,985	3K	44,812
36	101,831	97,883	3K	52,593
37	112,014	107,672	3K	61,152
38	123,216	118,439	3K	70,568
39	135,537	130,283	3K	89,924
40	149,091	143,311	3K	92,317
41	164,000	157,642	3K	104,849
42	180,400	173,407	3K	118,634
43	198.440	190,747	3K	133,797
44	218,284	209,822	3K	150,477
45	240,113	230,804	3K	168,825
46	264,124	253,885	3K	189,007
47	290,537	279,273	3K	211,208
48	319,591	307,201	3K	235,629
49	351,550	337,921	3K	262,491
50	386,705	371,713	3K	292,041
51	425,375	408,884	3K	324,545
52	467,913	449,773	3K	360,299
53	514,704	494,750	3K	399,629
54	566,175	544,225	3K	442,892
55	622,792	598,648	3K	490,482
56	685,071	658,513	3K	542,830
57	753,578	724,364	3K	600,413
58	828,936	796,800	3K	663,754
59	911,830	876,480	3K	733,430
60	1,003,013	964,128	3K	810,073
61	1,103,314	1,060,541	3K	894,380
62	1,213,646	1,166,596	3K	987,118
63	1,335,011	1,283,255	3K	1,089,130
64	1,468,512	1,411,581	3K	1,201,343
65	**$1,615,363**	**$1,552,739**		**$1,324,777**
Total Invested	$15,000	$24,000		$117,000
Total Earnings	$1,600,363	$1,528,739		$1,207,777

The Fiscally Fit Millionaire's chart shows what investing $3,000 a year will do based on 10% interest compounded monthly. The person who starts saving early will yield bigger returns than the person who starts saving later, though they pay in more years. If a fifteen-year-old were to invest $3K a year for five years and then never invest another dime, he would still have more money at age fifty than the "late" investor who invests $3K a year starting at age nineteen and invests for eight years. And the "late" investor will have more than the "later" investor who begins investing at age twenty-seven and invests for thirty-nine years. It's simple math, and it's simply astounding! This is an important teaching tool that can be used with your children to get them to invest early—just show them the numbers. It's still not too late for most of you either! Take a peek at the chart below to see where you could eventually arrive.

A DOLLAR A DAY
CUMULATIVE RETURN

Years	Total Invested	5%	10%	15%	20%
10	$3,600	$4,658	$6,145	$8,257	$11,283
20	7,200	12,331	22,781	44,917	93,290
30	10,800	24,968	67,815	207,698	689,335
40	14,400	45,781	189,722	930,482	5,021,546
50	18,000	80,060	519,732	4,139,793	36,509,163

Five Habits of Highly Effective Millionaires

So what are the habits of your average millionaire? Let's look at five that can make all the difference.

HABIT #1
THE MINDSET "EARN-TO-SPEND-LESS"

According to Michael LeBouef, author of *Finding the Millionaire in You* (msn.com, 9/8/2003, Barbara Reinhold), many wealthy people live simply rather than living in expensive homes. They opt for financial independence rather than outward appearances.

The average lotto winner, or any person who gets "easy" money, almost never values those dollars. In fact, more than 90% of those who win the lottery use up their money in less than ten years, and some manage to do it within a matter of weeks or months. But those who earn their money the hard way view it as something to save and invest rather than income to spend.

Habit #2
Focus

The focus of a millionaire, LeBouef says, is resisting the impulse to be scattered in your efforts and interests. "Winners focus; losers spray," he warns. It's easier to keep goals when we write them down. The people who consistently invest, as our chart indicates, are the ones who sacrifice the temporary for the long term. But you don't have to live an austere lifestyle in order to accomplish this. You only need to live below your means and invest the difference. Those who truly succeed in this investment goal will set up an automatic investment deduction from their paycheck—so that their investments happen before they even see the money. It's a lot easier to invest off the top. Then you don't miss it when you plan your monthly budget.

Live below your means and invest
the difference.

HABIT #3
DOING WHAT IT TAKES

Another characteristic of millionaires is that they are willing to do what it takes in order to meet their goals. People who garner millions over the course of their lives focus on the goal. They know what their mission is and are willing to sacrifice in order to meet their objective.

Jim and Sue McIntyre are millionaires profiled in David Bach's book *The Automatic Millionaire* (Broadway Books, 2004). Jim was a middle manager for a utility company and Sue was a hairdresser. This couple never made a combined income of more than $54,000 per year, and in the early years they made a lot less. By "doing what it takes" they were able to retire in their early fifties with a $450K home (paid for), a second home valued at $325K (paid for), and no debt. They owned two cars, a boat, and had a 401(k) valued at $610K, another retirement account valued at $72K, bonds totaling $160K, and $62K in cash in a savings account. Their net worth is around $2 million.

Early on the McIntyres decided to invest 10% of their income directly from their paychecks. They said, "You'd be surprised at how quickly you get used to doing without that 10%. And meanwhile it's piling up in the bank. The secret is that you can't spend what you don't see." They chose not "to do debt" and live comfortably while saving for their future.

My husband, Bob, and I follow much the same path that the McIntyres followed, but we also take it a step further and give 10%, or a tithe, to our local church, but more about that later in the chapter.

HABIT #4
TAKE CALCULATED RISKS

Barbara Reinhold, a career coach at Monster.com, says, "Perhaps it goes without saying, but you have to take strategic risks to earn and grow money. And a little rebelliousness seems to help too. One interesting study found that a majority of male millionaire entrepreneurs had been in trouble with school authorities or the police during their adolescent years. (So there's hope for parents of rebels.) Seriously, the mindset of these entrepreneurs is that it's all right to take a risk if you have weighed the pros and cons and you are confident that the risk is a wise money move. There are 100% guarantees in very few kinds of investments, but homework usually pays off when you are willing to take calculated, thoughtful risks."

HABIT #5
SHARING MATTERS

In my first book, *Shop, Save, and Share,* I wrote that the heart of the message was the "sharing" element, or being a provision to others in need. David Bach's final chapter in *The Automatic Millionaire* is entitled "Make a Difference With Automatic Tithing." Bach encourages readers to give 10% of their income away to nonprofit organizations. In an interview on PBS, Suze Orman was discussing the concept of tithing as found in her book *The Courage to Be Rich* (Penguin Putnam, 2001). She held her hand in a fist and said, "If you are so focused on clutching onto what you already have, you aren't open to receiving." And then she opened her hand to drive the point home.

More and more of the top financial experts are seeing the

value of giving away a part of their wealth in an effort to find balance in life. But it goes beyond being generous for tax breaks, it's for the pure joy of giving. According to the Merrill Lynch Cap-Gemini report, millionaires who live in North America are two to five times more likely to give to causes they value than are their European cousins. Yet they could give more. The average millionaire gives 3% to charity, which is much lower than the 5% most mainstream Americans give.

FISCAL FITNESS WORKOUT

THE "SHARING" CHALLENGE

So how do you learn to be generous when you realize this is a weak area of your potential millionaire-hood? I'm going to suggest some ways you can begin to enjoy the idea of sharing your time, resources, and finances. I challenge you to do follow-up on one item from this list each week for six weeks. You will find, especially if you haven't been very generous yet, that there is a tremendous feeling of satisfaction that walks alongside generosity. My challenge is simply this: I believe you will feel and live better after you develop the habit of giving. Try it for six weeks and let me know the results—I look forward to hearing from you!

You will feel and live better after you develop the habit of giving.

SIMPLIFY!

One of the best ways to help yourself and help others at the same time is to tackle a room, closet, or even a piece of furniture and clean it out. For example, you could choose to start in your bedroom and go through your dresser drawers. Take everything out of each drawer and put it in one of three piles: (1) give away; (2) throw away; and (3) keep. Call a nonprofit organization that needs and wants your donations—some of them will even come by to pick up your overages. In this cleaning-out process, you are helping to meet the needs of someone else in your community. If you do this with each room in your home, including the garage, not only will you relieve the clutter—you'll relieve stress in the process of helping others. Does it get any better than that?

Donate: Pay attention to information in your community about specific needs. This info might be through flyers, in the newspaper, posted on a bulletin board, or in your church's weekly program. Don't ignore these needs. Instead, dedicate fifteen minutes toward collecting specific items that are needed. It might be a matter of donating your soda cans, collecting food items, or gathering specific items of clothing. You might even want to add some of these things to your shopping list and donate new items. If you begin to develop the mindset of giving, the next time you hear of a need you won't be inclined to think, "Oh no! Not again!" Rather, you'll begin to think, "I wonder how I can meet this need in my own way?" You don't have to be extravagant; it really is true that every little bit helps.

Give Time: Our time is one of the most valuable commodities we have today, and it's a great equalizer: Donald Trump has the same twenty-four hours as you do! Why not look at donating your time to a nonprofit organization? You could plug into a monthly ministry at your church that takes food and clothing to Mexico or welcomes new people into the community. You might want to donate a couple of hours per month at a local food pantry or soup kitchen. This could be a great way to spend time with other family members if you do it together. Our family spends time gathering food and clothing donations for our local homeless shelter, and we deliver them in person. You might get hooked and decide you want to make an even greater time commitment and coach a soccer team, become a "Big Sister" or "Big Brother," or volunteer in a Scout program. If you're still stumped as to what you can do, go to *www.volunteer.com* to get more ideas. Giving time does not substitute for donating money to an organization, but it is something almost everyone can give.

> *Donald Trump has the same twenty-four*
> *hours as you do!*

Tithe on EVERYTHING

I found that when I began to hold our material goods in open palms rather than clenched fists, I found all kinds of opportunities to be generous. Once I got five free gourmet cookies on an airplane because I was inconvenienced by a delayed flight. I gave three of them to fellow passengers who hadn't had time to get lunch, and after all, cookies for lunch are better than no lunch at all—don't you think?

What about you? Here's a quick list of items you could give away. Why not try picking three and sharing them this next week:

Clothing
Food
Gifts
Cars (or give someone a ride)
The Use of Your Stuff (washer/dryer, a room for the night, lawn mower—Sorry guys! We'll return it, I promise!—your boat, pool, or camper)
Money
Time
Creativity
Talents
Encouraging Words
Books
Furniture
Appliances
Tools (even your Sears Craftsman tools with a life-time guarantee!)
Flowers
Cards
Hugs
Art
Chocolate (unless they are Godiva—then you'd better eat them ALL very quickly before they melt!)

You get the general idea. I've been able to give from every single one of these categories and the results are amazing. There was a time when one of my readers had the urge to give the school secretary a dozen roses that she received as a gift. She didn't know how to explain "why" she did it, just that she needed to do it. The secretary's eyes filled with tears as she said, "Since my divorce, I never receive flowers. This week was my birthday, and while I got some nice gifts, no one gave me flowers. But when you gave me these, it made me feel like everything will be all right."

I've heard from people who were challenged by my book *Shop, Save, and Share* and decided to give away their good used second car. In each case the feeling they got from meeting someone else's need was indescribable. Most families were also able to get a tax receipt for their donation when they gave vehicles to a nonprofit organization or routed the gift through their church or not-for-profit ministry.

Bring Peace to the World

Hope for Israel was founded in 2000 by our son-in-law, Moran Rosenblit. Moran was born and raised in Israel. During his service in the IDF (Israeli Defense Forces), he lost some close friends in a tragic event. As a result, he lost hope for life and for Israel.

In 1997 Moran arrived in the United States, seeking to find hope and a future. After accepting an invitation to visit Hope Chapel in Hermosa Beach, California, Moran was challenged by the pastor to seek truth for himself. As a result, Moran found a new hope, not only for his own life but also for Israel and the rest of the world.

Moran and our daughter Melissa now spend their lives sharing that hope by bringing a message of reconciliation between man and man as well as between man and God. For more information, go to *www.hope4israel.org* or support this ministry of reconciliation at:

Hope for Israel
Hope Chapel
P.O. Box 385
Redondo Beach, CA 90277

ADOPT A THIRD-WORLD CHILD

When asked why they don't sponsor a child, most families will say that they can't be certain their money really goes to that child. You can go to the BBB Wise Giving Alliance at *www.give.org* for a "Better Business Bureau Wise-Giving Guide." This will help you decide which organization to choose. Most sponsorships run anywhere from $25 to $35 per month and provide food, clothing, housing, and education to children. We've had the thrill of watching kids grow up under our sponsorship and go out to become leaders in their communities. Currently our family sponsors children from three reputable organizations:

- *World Vision*—On their "Ways to Give" link, you can choose where you want your dollars to go. They help children in the United States as well as around the world. Go to *www.worldvision.org* or call 1–888–511–6598.
- *Compassion International*—This is an organization that is tuned into crisis and special needs as well as the general monthly needs of children around the world. They encourage communication with your child, and you have the chance to see photos and read about how your child is doing in

school. It's a great project for your family.

• *Mission of Joy*—This is a lesser-known organization that was started by two Air Force captains when they saw the needs in India. Almost 97% of the monthly contributions go directly to India, because the ministry uses volunteer help and has very little overhead. Go to *www.missionjoy.org* or e-mail the founder at *Jeffreyoleary@jeffoleary.com*.

JOIN YOUR LOCAL CHURCH

If you are not a part of a local church, you and your family are missing out on some incredible opportunities. According to Barna Research online (*www.barna.org*), Americans believe in the power and impact of prayer: More than four out of five adults (82%) pray during a typical week. Four out of five (82%) believe "Prayer can change what happens in a person's life." Nine out of ten adults (89%) agree, "There is a God who watches over you and answers your prayers." Almost nine out of ten people (87%) say that the universe was originally created by God. Clearly, most Americans are open to the idea of God. Are you? Then why not find a church that meets your family's unique spiritual needs. Once you find your fit, partner with them financially so that you can reach your community with God's love.

Trade Tricks to Make Saving Easy

In summary, it's easy to talk about the habits of millionaires, but how do you put these actions into practice? Doing these things sound like a good idea, but coming up with the cash seems to be a lot harder. But if you are smart and savvy, it doesn't have to be all that difficult.

TRADE TRICK #1:
PUTTING EXTRA PAYCHECKS INTO SAVINGS

If you are paid every two weeks, there will always be two extra paychecks for you each year. There will come a month when you will get three paychecks instead of two. If you're paid weekly, there will be fifty-two checks per year, and some months you'll get five paychecks instead of four. At the beginning of the year, sit down and take ten minutes to figure out when you are getting these "extra" paychecks. Then purpose to put any extra checks into your savings account. Barbara O'Neill, author of *Savings on a Shoestring* (Dearborn Trade Publishers, 1996) says, "Your major expenses won't change from month to month. So if you can afford them in those months where you get two (or four) paychecks, you should be able to afford them when you get three (or five)."

TRADE TRICK #2: AUTOMATE

If No. 1 doesn't sound like your cup of tea, just divert 10% of your net pay automatically into your savings account during each pay period and live on the rest. Pat Jennerjohn, a certified financial planner, says, "Once you see your savings build, you'll be less likely to pull money out because you'll become attached to the higher balance."

For a start, the Consumer Credit Counseling Service says that every family should have three to six months of savings set aside in order to bridge possible gaps in employment and keep unexpected major expenses off of credit cards.

"Every family should have three to six months of savings set aside."

TRADE TRICK #3: GET BONDED FOR LIFE

Some employers allow their employees to purchase savings bonds with as little as $25 from their checks. Some of these bonds are paying more than savings accounts or CDs. To get a jump on these kinds of savings, go to *www.easysaver.gov* or *www.savingsbonds.gov*. These "little" bonds could add up to big bucks in the long run.

TRADE TRICK #4: "CHANGE"-ING YOUR LIFE

David Bach, author of *Smart Women Finish Rich* (Broadway, 2002), made oodles of money by promoting his "Latte Factor." He said that with as little as what you'd spend on a latte, invested over year, you could end up being rich. If you took your change and threw it into a jar, adding a few dollars here and there, you could easily invest $100 per month. The secret would be to avoid hitting the ATM every time you feel a bit short-changed.

TRADE TRICK #5: TIPS FROM A COUPON QUEEN

I've helped thousands of families learn to cut their food budgets in half. But what good does that do a family if they don't do something productive with the savings? It could easily be absorbed back into the monthly spending if there isn't a real plan for those savings. I suggest you take whatever money you save from coupons and immediately write a check into your savings account for that amount. This way, your monthly food budget stays the same, but your savings account will be on the rise.

TRADE TRICK #6:
LET UNCLE SAM LINE YOUR POCKETS

The "NRF 2004 Tax Returns Consumer Intentions and Actions Survey" conducted by BIGresearch for the National Retail Federation (NRF), found that 67.6% of consumers, or 145.7 million people, expect to receive a tax refund this year. The Internal Revenue Service announced that the average tax return as of March was $2,182, up 4.4% from $2,089 last year at that time. Though many consumers plan to use their refund checks to pay down debt (49.2%) or add to their savings (37.4%), others will use their refund for everyday expenses (27%), to make a major purchase (11.6%), or for vacation (12.2%). If you're not paying down debt, the most important thing you can do with your refund is to put it into savings.

You can also get a tax credit of up to $1,000 for contributions you make to a traditional IRA, a Roth IRA, a 401(k), or a 403(b), says enrolled agent David Mellem. This credit could be used to reduce the amount of tax you pay, or it could increase your refund. Make sure you are getting this benefit if you qualify for it and decide that you're going to save it. For more information, read IRS Form 8880.

The point of this chapter is not "How to Become a Millionaire in Ten Easy Steps" but rather to inspire you with an overview of how easy it is to let compounded interest work for you.

There's never been a better day to start saving for the future than today. Why not stop for a moment, grab a pen and paper, get a cup of coffee (and those Godiva chocolates you *won't* share), and sit back for a moment. Decide upon three action points you can take away from this chapter. Pick one significant way you can be generous or share this week and two more ways you can kick your savings up to the next level. Writing your goals down makes them more likely to happen, and they reinforce your resolve. Enjoy!

CHAPTER SIX

New Health Trends
The FICO Approach to Fiscal Fitness

Have you ever been around people who are trying to be "honest" but end up dishing out a brutal honesty that makes you want to go home and throw yourself under the covers and not come out for a month? Those in the public eye have to deal with this kind of "commando honesty" frequently—but it's not necessarily a bad thing because it keeps us on our toes. Pam, a friend of mine, recently completed a successful speaking event to a very large audience. When the meeting concluded, Pam came down from the podium and was greeted by a long line of women eager to express their gratitude for her inspiring talk. After the initial rush was over, a woman who had been lurking behind the others walked up to her and looked her up and down.

"You know, Pam," she said, "I used to be in awe of you before I saw you in person. But now I see that you're a real person just like anyone else."

Pam was flattered and responded, "Well . . . thank you so much!"

But the woman didn't stop there. She *should* have stopped there. Pam really *wished* the gal would have stopped there. Unfortunately, she didn't.

She pointed at Pam's stomach and declared, "I mean, you're so real that you even have a little pooch right there!"

Pam was shocked, but she maintained her composure. She was used to some of the strange comments that come from well-meaning audience members, and she graciously replied, "Bless your heart."

The next month Pam was at another event and was approached by a woman during the break.

"Pam," said the lady, "when I first saw your photo on the brochure, I thought, 'Now, what in the world could I learn from a young blonde like this?' But I'm happy to report that I've learned you're not as ditzy as you look."

The veteran speaker was composed and gave her standard response to strange remarks: "Bless your heart."

$ $ $

So I'm passing on this bit of wisdom to you, and it may just turn out to be one of the most helpful bits of advice in this book. The next time your mother-in-law asks, "Honey, are you gaining weight—*again?*" Just smile sweetly and say, "Bless your heart!"

There are times when I want to "bless the heart" of some of the people I run into. For example, a couple of months ago I went for an annual checkup at the doctor's office. The nurse seemed to take great pleasure in telling me I'd gained weight and my cholesterol wasn't as low as it was previously. But these are numbers we need to know whether we want to know them or not. To remain ignorant about these numbers could negatively affect our physical health.

There are, in fact, two numbers every person needs to know

in order to remain physically healthy. The first is their weight, which is the most obvious number, and most Americans have a general idea of how much they weigh. The second number is their cholesterol level. But fewer Americans know what their cholesterol number is.

There is a third and final number you need to know, and it may surprise you a bit. It's your FICO score, and it has nothing to do with your physical health and everything to do with your financial health. It is your credit score, and while over 90% of Americans know what a FICO *is*, only 33% know what their personal score is.

Basically, your credit score is the number that is calculated from data in your credit report. These scores help lenders make fairer credit decisions, since they reveal facts to them that relate to your general credit risk. The factors involved in the rating are based purely on the numbers and not on race, religion, nationality, gender, or marital status. While some people assume that these last two factors (gender and marital status) are credit risk factors, that is a misconception.

While some women may not have as good credit scores as their male counterparts, it usually has more to do with whether they have established a credit history of their own and developed good credit rather than from joint accounts. Many women do not realize that their individual FICO score is a different number from their husband's. Each has a separate rating. It is true that in the case of joint credit, the factors involved will affect both spouses, but the individual numbers are still separate.

Unfortunately, there are groups of women who have not realized the importance of cultivating their own good FICO score. If they find themselves in a situation where their spouse is suddenly out of the picture (due to death or divorce) they may feel the ramifications of a low FICO when they venture into the world alone. It's important for everyone, male or female, single or married—-to know how to improve their FICO and use it as a tool to make it work for them.

I receive a lot of questions about this topic when I speak, and in my inbox, so let's look at some of the most common concerns:

WHY DO I NEED A GOOD FICO SCORE?

A good credit score is invaluable to every American. Here are the benefits of a good score in a nutshell:

- *Loans*—A good credit score helps you qualify for loans and get faster loan approval.
- *Interest Rates*—Your FICO score is often the determining factor when it comes time for a lender to give you an interest rate. A better rating can help you get a better mortgage rate and could even make the difference between becoming a homeowner rather than a renter.
- *0% APR*—Have you ever been tempted by the advertisement on a new car, furniture, or a new credit card that offers a special "0% APR"? Do interest rates get any better than that? No wonder so many people line up to sign up for these special deals. But wait a minute! No so fast! Few people realize that these kinds of special offers only go to those who have the top levels in the national distribution of FICO scores.
- *So Close and Yet So Far*—Sometimes the difference between qualifying for a great deal and not qualifying for it can be as close as twenty points on your FICO score. You may say, "So

what? I don't qualify for it. I can still qualify for a fairly low interest rate." Well, it really does add up, and it matters a great deal. The difference on a $20K car loan at a 0% APR versus the standard 7% to 8% APR is around $1,800 over the course of the loan. This is very significant indeed!

- *Insurance Rates*—Does having a bad credit rating affect anything other than loans and interest rates? YES, it could affect what kind of insurance premium you will pay. According to Bankrate.com, staff writer Lucy Lazarony writes, "Some auto insurers are using credit data to help determine your insurance rates. Ninety-two of the one hundred largest personal auto insurance companies in the country use credit data in underwriting new business, according to a study by Conning & Company, an insurance research and asset management firm."

> *"A consumer with bad credit is going to pay 20% to 50% more in auto insurance premiums than a person who has good credit."*

There does seem to be a connection between your credit score and the likelihood of your having to file an auto insurance claim. It's purely in the numbers. According to a study by the Insurance Information Institute, drivers at the bottom of the credit chart file 40% more claims than drivers at the top. Clarence Smith, assistant vice-president at Conning & Company, says, "A consumer with bad credit is going to pay 20% to 50%

more in auto insurance premiums than a person who has good credit."

If you're already insured, you might want to stay where you are—especially if your credit is not what it could be. Insurance underwriters follow the credit data when reviewing new customers, and far fewer (only 14%) national insurers use credit data for renewals. In fact, some states don't allow this practice at all.

I Know That My FICO Is My Credit Number, But What Is a FICO, Anyway?

Your credit number is called "FICO" because most credit bureau scores use formulas developed by Fair Isaac Corporation.® These scores are provided to the three major credit reporting agencies: Equifax, Experian, and TransUnion. As they process the data differently, there may be a slight difference in these scores from each reporting agency, but they are usually within a few points of each other.

FICO scores provide the best guide to the kind of credit risk you will be to lenders. They figure that if you have a higher score, you're going to be a lesser risk than if you have a lower score. This doesn't mean you will be perceived as a good or bad customer; it's just what the statistics are saying about your financial habits, including available credit, payment history, and credit-to-debit ratios.

There's not a magic number that will guarantee you will get a better interest rate or that you automatically become a low-risk borrower. These numbers are somewhat subjective as they vary from lender to lender. One lender may feel you need to have a 700-or-above rating to qualify for their card, whereas another lender's cutoff point may be around 550. That's why when you're shopping for loans, you need to get quotes from a variety of lenders.

What Do Different FICO Scores Look Like in Terms of a Mortgage Loan?

Below is a chart comparing FICO scores and interest rates on a $150,000 home loan for a 30-year, fixed-rate mortgage:

FICO Score	Interest Rate	Monthly Payments
720–850	5.488%	$851
700–719	5.613%	$862
675–699	6.151%	$914
620–674	7.301%	$1,028
560–619	8.531%	$1,157
500–599	9.289%	$1,238

You can see from this chart how having a good score can not only make the difference between buying the kind of home you want but can also make the difference between whether you qualify for a mortgage and can begin to build wealth through home ownership.

How Does My FICO Score Stack Up to the National Average?

National distribution of FICO scores

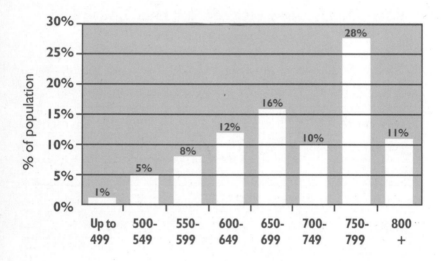

You'll see that 28% of all Americans have a very good score of 750–799 with 11% at the highest range of 800+. Only 5% fall into the 500–549 range and 8% into the 550–599 range.

Could a Low Score Mean I'll Be Denied Credit?

The only absolute for credit is that there are no absolutes! While a high FICO makes it reasonable to assume you'll get a particular loan, it doesn't guarantee it any more than a low score will guarantee that you won't get the loan. There are a number of factors involved, including your ability to repay the debt, your credit history, and your employment status and history. Here are the "greatest hits" on FICOs or the items that most negatively impact your credit score:

- Late payments
- Bankruptcies
- Collections

Is the Current Method of Credit Scoring Unfair to Minorities?

Yes and no. As I mentioned earlier, a woman who does not establish good credit lines on her own and only has co-credit with her spouse may be negatively impacted upon widowhood or divorce. Women who are not the primary providers in the home may have the same problems due to inattention to individual personal credit lines. But as a whole, the credit scoring process is impartial, and the ECOA (Equal Credit Opportunity Act) prohibits lenders from discriminating or considering consumers based on their race, gender, nationality, or marital status.

Will My Score Take a Dip if I Apply for New Credit?

Applying for new credit should only affect you in a negative way if you open multiple accounts, securing multiple loans simultaneously. For example, let's say you get your dream job with a substantial pay raise and you relocate to a much lower cost of living area. You could easily buy a new home, new car, and new wardrobe. You decide to get some new clothes right away because that seems like the easiest way to celebrate. The salesperson tells you that you can get a 15% discount on that new suit if you open a store charge account, and you think, "I can cancel this after I get it, but that 15% is really going to add up on all these clothes I'm buying for my new job." This same pattern is repeated at several stores, and you're jazzed about saving so much money with this clever store credit card trick.

Then you go to the car dealership with your friend who is good at negotiating and get a great price on a new car and a super-duper interest rate on the loan. Finally it's time to go buy your dream home, and since you were told you had a good FICO when you started looking several months ago, you've figured out how much house you can afford at the interest rate you should be able to qualify for. The only problem is that your FICO used to be great, but it's taken a significant hit due to all the credit cards you've opened, the new car you just bought, and the credit inquiries into your account for your new insurance policy. Suddenly your very manageable mortgage payment that you estimated at $851 per month is now going to be a whopping $1,028 per month due to the fact that you now have a lower FICO score.

So Which Loans Should I Secure First if I'm Going to Get Multiple Loans?

While one new account may only moderately hit your FICO, multiple accounts for greater debt will hit it hard. Consequently, here is the order in which you should apply for these loans in order to maximize your credit rating and get the best interest rate on the largest loans:

1. Your mortgage loan
2. Your car
3. Other accounts (including credit cards and the establishing of utilities such as electricity, gas, and water)

Are You Saying That a Lower FICO Score Could Raise the Cost of My Utilities?

When we recently bought a new home in California and had not yet sold our home in New Mexico, we ran into the problem of a dropping FICO score. We had excellent FICO scores, enough to carry two mortgages on two homes, and we were able to get the best mortgage rate possible. But without my knowledge, my husband had taken out a 0% APR loan for a hot tub cover and some furniture. We had agreed to set aside the money to make these purchases, and we had the ability to pay the debt immediately. But when Bob walked into the store, his thought process was *Why not use someone else's money for a year instead of our own? We can keep our money in investments and come out ahead.*

He wasn't aware of how multiple accounts hit a FICO. By the time we secured first and second mortgages and lines of credit for the consumer goods, we were told that we had to pay a deposit on our electricity setup because Bob's credit rating was not as high as it needed to be in order to waive the deposit!

Consequently, we had to set up the services in my name, under my FICO score, because I had guarded my credit rating and didn't have the additional lines of credit open. It can happen to any of us if we're not aware of the factors involved in FICO scoring.

You Keep Talking About the "Factors" Involved in Credit Scoring—What Are These?

There are five basic categories that influence your score:

- **Time:** This is the length of your credit history and the amount of time since your accounts were opened. These are viewed and ranked by specific types of accounts.

- **New Credit:** This is the number of recently opened accounts as well as the number of inquiries into your credit history. This would also include the reestablishment of credit after a bad credit history.
- **Type:** There are five basic kinds of credit accounts: credit cards, mortgage loans, store (or retail) cards, consumer finance accounts, and installment loans (including car loans).
- **Debt Load:** This is the number of accounts you have and the proportion of revolving debt to the total amount of credit lines available. These are called debt ratios, and we will discuss these in detail in the next section.
- **History:** This primarily means your payment history, including whether you pay on time, how much you pay down on revolving debt (or do you only pay the minimums), your payment patterns, whether you've defaulted on loans, and any other bankruptcies or delinquencies. The last three entries will be removed from your credit history after a certain period (usually five to seven years).

Here is what it looks like:

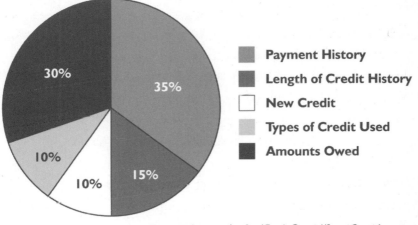

Payment History
Length of Credit History
New Credit
Types of Credit Used
Amounts Owed

www.myfico.com/myfico/CreditCentral/ScoreConsiders.asp

How to Have Your Piece of the Pie

If you have a good FICO score, there's a way to keep it that way. And there is also good news if you currently have a bad FICO score—there is room for improvement, and it may happen more quickly than you would think. Here are the basic steps to an improved FICO score:

Pay on Time: As you read in chapter 4, some credit cards may have a cycle of as little as twenty-one days, so pay your minimum as soon as you get your bill (and send more later) or set it up with your bank to automatically pay the credit card company every month.

Check Your Credit: Each month your credit card bill will come in, and the first thing you need to do is to check it for discrepancies. Not only is this an early indicator of possible identity theft, but it also allows you to make sure you're not being tapped with erroneous charges. If you find a discrepancy, it's important to contact the lender or a credit bureau as soon as possible.

Debt Ratios: Part of your scoring depends upon what your debt ratio is—or the amount of debt versus the total amount of credit available to you. According to Bankrate.com,

> Credit-scoring models look at a number of factors when calculating your score, including the result of the following formula: the total amount of debt on credit cards and revolving accounts divided by the total amount of debt available on those accounts. The formula results in a fraction less than one. The lower the fraction, the better. A score of one would mean your outstanding debt equals your available credit and you've maxed out your credit cards.

An example would be an available credit line of $10,000 and $5,000 in debt. When you divide the total credit by the debt, you have a ratio of one-half. You are using one-half of the credit available to you. But if you're using a card with a credit line of $15,000 and you still carry the $5,000 in debt, you have a better ratio of one to three or one-third of the credit available to you.

If you are going to buy an automobile or a home, the best

advice regarding your debt ratio would be to pay down as much debt as you can and not to cancel these lines of credit until after you've secured your larger loan.

Time: Time can be a good thing when it comes to your FICO score; not only can you improve it over time, but the longer you've had a card, the higher your credit limit is (which helps the ratios we discussed in the previous point), and it also proves a solid credit history. So if you need to cancel a credit card, hang on to those you've had the longest and those that have the highest credit limit. When you have a history of paying your bills on time, paying down revolving balances, and not biting off more debt than you can chew, then you will see a steady increase in your FICO number.

Limit Inquiries: Most consumers are not aware of the fact that each time a potential lender inquires into your credit history, you take a hit on your FICO score. This is because a large number of inquiries over a short period of time may indicate that you are opening too many credit accounts due to financial difficulties, such as unemployment or an unexpected financial setback. It could also indicate that you are taking on more debt than you can comfortably pay back.

There's a good chance that you've just gained new knowledge about how FICO scores work and how they can be used as an effective tool in helping your family get what they need without going into greater debt and becoming a "servant to the lender." Why not go a step further and allow the take-away portion of this chapter to be something you can act on this week?

Write down your goals for improving your FICO and take one step a week for the next six weeks, tracking your FICO as you go along to see the improvement. You may be pleasantly surprised at the positive results and feel more empowered to be in control of your debt weight than ever before. Just do me a favor: Don't go out and charge a new suit to celebrate—pay cash instead!

CHAPTER SEVEN

The Sixty-Minute Money Workout

A Guide to a Fight-Free Zone for Couples

"When choosing between two evils, I always like to try the one I've never tried before." —Mae West

Some couples may feel like Mae West when it comes to the idea of a "discussion" of money matters. Justin and Betty, a couple I counseled, said, "We would either fight over money or let the tension simmer under the surface while we carefully avoided the topic." Lenn Furrow, a counselor friend who works for a major government family support center, said, "Most couples would rather discuss problems in their sex life than discuss their finances."

David Berky, a writer for a wonderful Web site called SimpleJoe.com, said, "It has been estimated that half of all divorces occur to some degree because of disagreements over money and finances." The statistics agree with Berky's assessment. "Money problems" are cited as the primary reason for divorce in 51% of the cases.

But as odd as it sounds, conflicts over money are not always about money, according to Jack Otter, with *SmartMoney* magazine. A new survey conducted by both *SmartMoney* and *Redbook* magazines shows that money is really a control issue between couples. Otter says, "It's not just what you're buying, but it's who gets to decide what you're buying." Here are some of the results of the survey, taken from "Investing in America: Spending Survey" (for the complete results, go to *money.know-more.com/MONEY*):

Amnesia and Price Tags: Many couples don't come clean about their spending, and even those that are honest aren't always *completely* honest about *exactly how much* they spend. Some 36% of men admit to fudging on the price of an item while 40% of women claim the item cost less than it actually did.

Money Baggage: Perhaps the most emotional and divisive arguments tend to occur in blended families with children from a previous marriage. Since that group represents such a large number of people, let's take a closer look. According to Otter, "The issues of how to handle the finances from the children of their previous marriage were hard to resolve because they already had a routine with their children." There is also the added factor of child support, legal expenses, and other monetary issues that magnify the money problems found in blended families.

One Checkbook or Two?: The majority of couples keep joint accounts, but 14% keep all accounts separate, while 18% have both joint and separate accounts.

Timing Is Everything: This fascinating survey indicated that most couples discussed their finances under the worst possible conditions—when they were tense and frustrated. It's no huge surprise to realize that most of these "discussions" (we call them fights at our house) were not resolved in a satisfactory manner.

These survey results are not surprising or revelatory, but they are worth looking at. In fact, they are the main reason I developed the "Sixty-Minute Money Workout," so that you can have a purposeful time discussing money *and* an effective tool to maximize the discussion without fighting or wishing you were having a root canal rather than a discussion about money.

Here's a mini-quiz to see if you are a candidate for the "The Sixty-Minute Money Workout" approach to finances:

1. Are money arguments the No. 1 cause of disagreements in your home?
2. Do you seem to disagree more than you agree on your finances?
3. Do you instantly feel tension over the mere thought of talking money issues with your mate?
4. Do you seem to misunderstand the majority of the financial principles involved in household finances? Does your mate?
5. Would you say that either you or your mate tend to behave selfishly (either regularly or frequently) when it comes to money?
6. Would you rather your mate understand your perspective on money rather than understanding your mate first?
7. Do you think that winning the lottery, inheriting a small fortune, or getting a dream job with a dream salary would solve your financial problems?
8. Do you have trouble expressing financial goals?
9. Do you have enough patience to have a complete and honest discussion about finances?

10. Would you rather baby-sit teething triplets with a stomach virus than discuss finances?

If you answered yes to two or more of these questions, you are a prime candidate to greatly improve your marriage by improving your ability to discuss money issues. This workout is very much like the physical workout you have at the gym or when you hit the treadmill at "Home Sweet Home." Well, it *can* be sweet, if you follow my workout! When it comes to exercise, you're not going to be able to run a marathon after your first workout or enter a "Mr. Universe" contest after lifting a 100-pound barbell for ten reps and two sets! But if you've ever gotten into the habit of getting fit, then you know that over the course of a few months, you begin to feel stronger (and look smashing)! The same is true of the money workout—you'll get hooked on the payoffs (literally!) of your hard work and be ready to leave your bad spending habits in the dust.

As you get used to how each exercise is designed to achieve the best results, you'll soon find that you and your mate are making progress: You're going to be able to discuss money without fighting, and you'll begin to solve some of your financial problems in the process. The first big hurdle will be finding time to have this workout and sticking to it when you don't "feel" like it. Just as you need to take safety precautions when entering any kind of physical exercise, such as wearing gloves for weight-lifting or the right kind of shoes for Pilates, you also need to set the scene for a healthy financial workout. Here are the ground rules.

GROUND RULES

A Refreshing Walk—Not a Marathon: One of the reasons most couples fight about money is that they feel they have to solve their problems in one sitting. This makes as much sense as trying to run the L.A. Marathon with a two-mile running base. Solving your problems will not happen in one marathon session. Simply learning to dialog on a difficult topic will be a giant step forward. The main consideration for optimum results from this workout is: Keep the discussion moving. You are learning to dialog, without strife, on a difficult topic.

Get in Sync: It's important to have these workouts scheduled into your week or month. Set aside an hour to go through each exercise and make it a firm commitment that cannot be bumped at the slightest whim. I suggest you start out doing this twice a month and then work up to a weekly workout until your financial situation improves. Then you can progress to a "maintenance program" where you only meet once a month or once every other month.

Seek Professional Help: If you find that these exercises are not helping your marital relationship and you still find yourselves fighting about money issues, it may be time to call in a professional. To find a financial counselor in your area, contact the Association for Financial Counseling and Planning Education (AFCPE) at 614–485–9650. You can also check out the Web site at *www.afcpe.org*. Many large churches offer financial counseling for free or on a sliding scale based upon your income and situation.

Seek to Understand Before Being Understood: This is taken straight out of Stephen Covey's book *The Seven Habits of Highly Effective People* (Free Press, 1990). There's a reason why Covey sold a gazillion copies of his book. The principles work. One of the principles is "Seek to understand before being understood." In the emotionally explosive arena of money and matrimony, it's important to agree that you will try to understand what your spouse is saying before seeking to be understood. You do this with phrases such as "I hear you saying that . . ." and then repeating what you understood him/her to say. At that point, your spouse can confirm your understanding or correct it. Here's an example:

> WILMA: "Fred, I'm currently spending $100 on dog food for Dino, and I want to buy it in bulk from Sam's Club so we can save about 50% of that each month. But we need to join the club first."
>
> FRED: "Okay, so you're saying you want to join Sam's Club and make me go broke by saving money!"
>
> WILMA: "No, it only costs $35 a year, and that isn't going to make us go broke; we can even shop there together and agree on our purchases. I hear they have great prices on bowling balls."
>
> FRED: "Oh, okay, I get it! Yabba-Dabba-Do!"

The Patience Principle: Before you begin, agree to keep the discussion to one hour. Each of you should verbally agree to be patient with your partner. It's only for sixty minutes, and I have confidence that you can be patient that long. If you can't, then you may want to pick up a marriage therapy book to read along-side this one! Seriously, you may want to consider reading *The*

Language of Love or *Men Are Like Waffles and Women Are Like Spaghetti* by Bill and Pam Farrel (Harvest House, 2001). Just think of what Wilma would have said if she hadn't purposed to be patient with Fred. Their discussion could have ended up at an impasse.

"Win-Win" or "Agree to Disagree" Solutions: This is another "Coveyism." Any conflict can be resolved in one of several ways: one wins/the other loses; "no deal" resolution, where neither side wins; both sides win or you agree to disagree. In this case, you want to go with the win/win or agree-to-disagree solution. Purpose before the discussion starts that you will have one of these favorable results after each exercise in the workout.

No Condescension Allowed: When one of you makes a lame comment or reveals ignorance on a particular topic (and this will happen on both sides), it's imperative that enlightenment is made without talking down to the other person—remember, you're on the same team.

Ixne Ottenre: That's pig Latin for "nix rotten," a principle that should apply at all times in a financial discussion with your mate. That means there are no rotten ideas You and your spouse need to allow each other the freedom to express all kinds of ideas without fear of ridicule. In fact, I know of couples involved in this kind of workout that actually throw out some outrageously funny (even bizarre) ideas just to lighten the discussion and have fun with the process.

Goal—Interdependence: It's been said, "He who controls the finances, controls the home." The women I know who control all of the finances and give their husbands an allowance are not happy gals. I think most of these ladies have taken on the role by forfeiture—but boy, when they take it, they really do run with it! Conversely, after I wrote *A Woman's Guide to Family Finances*, I heard from hundreds of women who either never saw the value of learning about finances or never found it in a format they could easily understand. Some of these women were widowed or divorced and wished they had gained a working knowledge of money before they encountered a crisis. If you are a woman in this category, you'll be blessed to see what an incredibly beneficial role you play in your family's finances.

Remember that the end goal is *interdependence*, where both spouses have a working understanding of their finances and could stand alone if they needed to. This could work itself out in a variety of ways. In some families, one spouse pays the bills and the other balances the checkbook. In other families, the financially skilled partner handles the money, but briefs the spouse on the status and seeks input for any significant financial decisions.

> *Remember that the end goal is* interdependence, *where both spouses have a working understanding of their finances and could stand alone if they needed to.*

Honesty: It's important to be honest during these conversations. If you have a new suit in the closet that the credit card bill will reflect next month—let your spouse know. If you don't understand a term or concept—ask your spouse to explain it to you. If you become aware of uncomfortable feelings related to associations you make with money, try to express yourself in a nonjudgmental way. Take the example of Richard and Christin. During a money workout session, Richard balked at the idea of Christin buying a new coat for the winter.

> RICHARD: "You already have a coat that will work fine."
> CHRISTIN: "But that coat is out of style and I bought it three winters ago."
> RICHARD: "I don't get it. Your coat isn't really out of style and it has plenty of good years left in it."
> CHRISTIN: "Okay, here's how I feel. As you know, I grew up in a family where money was tight and I always had to wear my sister's hand-me-downs. My clothes were often ill-fitting and never in style. I vowed that when I grew up, I'd be able to buy decent clothes. Furthermore, I think that having a new coat every three years instead of yearly is a good compromise. I don't plan on buying a designer coat or being extravagant."
> RICHARD: "I didn't know that this purchase had an emotional association for you. Let's get you a new coat. We'll donate your old one to the women's shelter."

When Christin explained her feelings about the past, Richard was able to understand why it was so important to her to buy a new coat. His awareness of her feelings and of her fiscal/emotional history allowed him to respond compassionately. Not only did their finances benefit from this exchange but their marriage did too. They found the balance that worked for them and their budget while still meeting Christin's emotional needs.

Positive Reinforcement: The overwhelming majority of people like to be affirmed and have their good habits reinforced. Look for ways you can express gratitude to your spouse and the value you place on him/her. You might have to start small, especially if there's been a negative history of exchange when it comes to finances. But in time the affirmation of your spouse won't be hard to express and it might even create an attitude of gratitude in your entire family.

That's why it's important to stress the "I" statements, rather than the "you" verbiage. Here's another example from Fred and Wilma.

> FRED: "So, Wilma, what I hear you saying is that you need $100 more per month to buy Dino's dog food."
>
> WILMA: "No, Fred, I'm currently spending $100 on dog food for Dino, and I want to buy it in bulk from Sam's Club so we can save about 50% of that each month. I feel confident that I can save our family money by doing this and I want to get out of debt."
>
> FRED: "Okay, so you're saying you want to join Sam's Club, but I'm afraid we might go broke trying to save money. I feel this might just be another excuse to spend and that makes me nervous."
>
> WILMA: "Fred, we're out of time for this part of the Sixty-Minute Money Workout, so let me just say that I think we can place boundaries on our shopping at the Club—only buying items we know we'll use that we can't get cheaper from the grocery or department

store. I promise I won't violate those financial bound-aries."

One at a Time, Please: Your finances didn't get chaotic over-night, and they're not going to get organized in one hour either. Give yourself time to make progress. One way to accomplish this goal is to cover one topic per workout—not three or four. See the warm-up section of the exercise for ideas on goal-setting topics.

Timing: A final word before we go over the workout is to pick a good time for this discussion. The person who said, "Timing is everything" was *so* right! The best time for this fiscal workout is preferably when neither of you are stressed out from paying bills, having discovered that there's too much month left at the end of the paycheck. Worse still, don't approach the discussion on the day you're in a bad mood because you've discovered you've gained five pounds.

FISCAL FITNESS WORKOUT

THE ONE-HOUR MONEY WORKOUT

Set a timer for each section and immediately stop discussions (or throwing things) when the bell rings. Then go on to the next section.

1. Make Up Your Mind Warm-Up (5 minutes): As you know by now, when Bob and I got married, we had $40,000 in consumer debt. We were like many other young people who didn't realize the price we would pay for instant gratification.

We purposed to get out of debt and made immediate changes in our lifestyle to accomplish this. We also decided to tithe 10% of all we made. We ended up living on less than 25% of one income in order to accomplish these goals. Within two and a half years we were debt free! We made up our minds, prayed to God for His help, and found the strength we needed to make—and stick to—the decision to become debt free.

This warm-up part of the workout is where you make up your mind and *verbally* commit to a bottom line financial goal. (You will write them down later.) Here are some suggested areas that you could cover—at a rate of one per week.

> *Overall Goals*
> Budget
> Debt Management
> Task Division
> Spending Levels and Goals
> Savings
> Investments
> College for Kids
> Teaching Kids About Money
> Tax Strategies
> Vacation and Entertainment Expenses
> Ways to Cut Spending
> Giving

2. Couple Meeting Strength Training (10 minutes): It usually takes more than one partner to get a couple into serious debt. Even if one person does most of the spending, the other spouse usually enables the destructive behavior in some way.

This meeting is a time to write down goals *on paper* so that you will have a tangible and objective standard to work toward. The points you write down should include: (a) a topic; (b) a goal for that topic; (c) steps to take to achieve the goal; (d) delineation of who will do what in achieving the goal; (e) outside resources that could help reach the goal.

There is a worksheet on the following page to help you get started. Or, create your own.

GOAL SETTING

TOPIC: _____

Goal: _____

_____

_____

Steps to Achieve This Goal: Who Will Be Responsible:

1. _____   1. _____

2. _____   2. _____

3. _____   3. _____

4. _____   4. _____

5. _____   5. _____

Outside Resources to Help Reach This Goal:

_____

_____

TOPIC: _____

Goal: _____

_____

_____

Steps to Achieve This Goal: Who Will Be Responsible:

1. _____   1. _____

2. _____   2. _____

3. _____   3. _____

4. _____   4. _____

5. _____   5. _____

Outside Resources to Help Reach This Goal:

_____

_____

_____

3. Budget Burn (20 minutes): Even though your topic du jour may not be about a budget, it's important to keep a consistent dialog going about this topic. Little else will matter in reaching your financial goals if you cannot create a workable budget and stick to it. There are two basic kinds of budgets: a structured one and a general one. The structured one has twelve categories and set percentages for each category for those who enjoy structure and filling in squares. (For a sample copy of this, see my bestselling book *Shop, Save, and Share* or go to *www.crown.org* or *MSNMoney.com* for a budget tool.) The general category budget is less restrictive and easier for some families to stick to. This one is found in my book *A Woman's Guide to Family Finances*. Or, you can e-mail our offices (*wendywendler@elliekay.com* or *ellie@elliekay.com*) for a sample copy.

The important thing is to find the budgeting technique that works for you. It might not be the same method you've used in years past or the approach used by your parents or friends. You will make it uniquely yours—so that you have a better chance of succeeding at keeping it! Finalize and agree to your new budget. This may not seem like a lot of time on this topic, but you will be working on it—bit-by-bit—each time you have your financial workout. This topic tends to be the most divisive among couples, so be sure to set your timer and STOP the discussion once your twenty minutes are up.

Once you have a workable budget, you will spend this time patting yourselves on the back for what's working and tweaking what needs adjusting. You can also use this time to discuss specific ways to spend less in each of the budgeted categories.

4. Taking Your Heart Rate (20 minutes): This is the point where you get the facts on your goal topic. It could include credit and debt information so you can decide if you need to go to a professional financial counselor. Check your credit report and order a copy from any of the major credit bureaus: Equifax (1–800–685–1111); Experian (1–888–297–3742); or Trans-Union (1–800–888–4213). This report costs about $8. If you live in Colorado, Georgia, Maryland, Massachusetts, New Jersey, or Vermont, or if you've been denied credit before, you qualify for a free copy annually. Or, you can get one online, for the same fee, at MSN Money. Besides this book and my others, there are quite a few Web sites that can provide the information you need to achieve your goal. Try *www.motleyfool.com*; *www.simplejoe.com*; *www.crown.org*; *www.msnmoney.com*; or, find additional appropriate links at *www.elliekay.com.*

5. Congratulations Cool Down (5 minutes): Sit back and grab a glass of something cool to drink and reflect on all you've accomplished in just one hour! Keep in mind that you're building on what you've done so far and you're in it for the long haul so you can have a lean mean checkbook machine. Use this opportunity to thank your spouse for his/her patience, diligence, understanding, or any other characteristic or action that you particularly appreciated during this last hour.

CHAPTER EIGHT

Savings Factors

*Three Major Ways to Drop Debt and
Beef Up on Cash*

My nickname as a child was "Money Bags." I was blessed at an early age with the ability to make money, use less money, and save money. Just as Denise Austin is the weight-loss guru for average Americans, I've spent a good portion of my adult life teaching others how to become fiscally fit. There are always new ways to save some dough, and you may find some of these rather surprising. If you want to drop debt but beef up on savings, here are several ways to help you keep more of the hard-earned cash you earn and allow you to prosper in your relationships at the same time.

Debt Dropper #1: The High Price of Fighting About Money

In the previous chapter we looked at why people fight about money and a workout that will allow you and your mate to live in healthy harmony. In the beginning of this chapter, I want to get a little more specific about the *cost* of fighting about money and how you can minimize your risk in this area. Research indicates that couples who argue *the most* about money often get into destructive cycles. They end up accruing greater debt, and consequently they have less in savings. In other words, fighting about money can cost you money. Let's look at some examples of how this works with most couples as well as some solutions to the problem.

> HE SAYS: "I make a good living, why can't I buy a new power tool if I want one?"
>
> SHE SAYS: "*Want* is the operative word here. You don't use the power tools you have now! In fact, you *need* a new gizmo about as much as I need a Tonco Rotisserie and BBQ!"
>
> HE SAYS: "Um . . . but you already *have* a Tonco Rotisserie and BBQ!"

> DOSE OF REALITY: The fact is, everyone likes to spend money on non-necessities with a certain amount of freedom. You may have a better grip on this kind of spending than your spouse does, but the desire to spend money the way you want to is human nature—it neither makes you good or bad, it just makes you human. It is what you do with this desire that counts.

> DEBT-DROPPER PLAN: If this "luxury spending" is budgeted into your monthly allocations, there's no need to fight over how this money is used. You may choose to buy a spa session, and your spouse may choose to have a different flavor of Jelly Belly® delivered to his doorstep each month. You stay relaxed; he feels like a kid again. What's not to love?

HE SAYS: "We need to fund our ROTH IRAs before we make any other kind of investment or expenditure."

SHE SAYS: "But you promised we could go to Hawaii this year!"

DOSE OF REALITY: According to Barbara Steinmetz, a financial planner in Burlingame, California, tension mounts between partners partly due to poor communication. "It usually happens because the two people involved aren't on the same page. One person thinks they have a shared goal of saving for a house, car, or retirement, while the other doesn't."

DEBT-DROPPER PLAN: Schedule a time to talk about your financial goals when you have a couple of hours of uninterrupted time and are relaxed. Purpose to go for the "win/win" deal in which each of you shares ownership in the development of an overall savings plan. Instead of making the goal an "*either/or*" situation, strive for a creative way to save for *both*.

HE SAYS: "I didn't really pay that much money, it's just a *little* Harley that I ordered. At least the helmet was on sale!"

SHE SAYS: "I saw the payment booklet, honey. If we only pay the minimums, it will take five or six years to pay off your 'little' spending spree!"

HE SAYS: "Does this mean you don't want to go for a ride?"

DOSE OF REALITY: This is an age-old problem that began when Eve was willing to risk paying the price for that piece of fruit and convinced her husband to ante up also. The fact is that in most marriages one spouse is a born spender and the other is a born saver, which sets the stage for the sparks to fly and the savings account to dwindle.

DEBT-DROPPER PLAN: It's important that the born saver not judge the born spender harshly. The best way to help a spender's buying habits come into balance is to sit down and develop a *workable* family budget. If you've "been there, done that" and it still isn't working, then do it again—in front of a family counselor who is familiar with principles of household budgeting. Just like food diets, you'd be surprised at how a little accountability can help keep you from cheating on your debt diet.

HE SAYS: "If we just give our son whatever he wants when he wants it, he'll never learn about money. So I told him he could earn half of the money for his new bike, and once he's earned his part, we'll give him the other half."

SHE SAYS: "Well, uh, this afternoon I bought him that bike. As a matter-of-fact, he's riding it now. And as he rode off into the sunset he called out, 'You're the best mom in the whole wide world!'"

DOSE OF REALITY: Most parents feel a responsibility to teach their kids to grow in their personal faith, say no to drugs and alcohol, and abstain from premarital sex. But they don't talk about the topic that is cited as the No. 1 reason for divorce—money issues. Raising a money-savvy kid will greatly heighten his odds for having a successful marriage one day.

DEBT-DROPPER PLAN: As a mom of seven, I know the challenge of teaching kids about money. My book *Money Doesn't Grow on Trees: Teaching Kids the Value of a Buck* was birthed out of that experience. The key is to make learning about money a pleasurable experience. Try using my "Fun Kid Budgets" at restaurants, the zoo, or theme parks. Calculate what it will cost for the meal (or event) and add a pad. Then tell your child you will give her a "budget" of this amount that is now her money to spend as she wishes. Plus she gets to keep what she doesn't spend! It's amazing how conservative a child becomes when she's not spending Mom and Dad's money, but her own.

HE SAYS: "I'm overdrawn again on my checking account and need you to make the house payment from your account."

SHE SAYS: "You have got to be kidding. We agreed on which bills I'd pay and which you would pay. My account shouldn't be penalized because you can't tell the difference between a Washington and a Jefferson!"

DOSE OF REALITY: Most marriages lose money when they have two checkbooks rather than one because they cannot see the big financial picture at a glance at any time. The "his money" and "her money" approach lends itself to arguments and additional expense.

DEBT-DROPPER PLAN: The best money-saving approach is to remember that the relationship isn't designed to be dependent or independent as much as it was created to be interdependent. If extenuating circumstances require two checkbooks, then create a mutual account for major household expenses so you'll both know your financial overview at any moment.

HE SAYS: "I just balanced the checkbook—or tried to. You hit the ATM so many times, I'm amazed your card didn't break in half! It says here that you got money on Friday, and today's Monday—how much of it do you still have?"

SHE SAYS: "Um . . . Nada. Zilch. Nothing. I don't really know where I spent it. Although I do remember going to the Starbucks by the mall."

DOSE OF REALITY: Ouch! Who hasn't "been there/done that"? Most people are not disciplined enough for the responsibility of multiple trips to the cash line. The more times you (or your spouse) visit the ATM or get cash back on a debit card—the more likely you are to end up cash poor.

DEBT-DROPPER PLAN: There's an old saying: "If you aim at nothing, you'll hit it every time." Decide you will limit your ATM or debit card withdrawals to a specific date and amount. If this boundary is violated, agree that the guilty party (who is now the party pooper) will take the additional money from their month's "luxury fund." When Party Pooper realizes she doesn't have enough saved to have the anticipated manicure, she will be much more inclined to keep her unmanicured index finger in her pocket the next time she passes by an ATM.

Debt Dropper #2: Insurance Assurance

What is one thing you need to have but hope you will never use?

Why, it's insurance, of course! Many insurance choices are "Pay me now or pay me later." Some families buy the wrong coverage and end up paying for their own losses, while others pay for more protection than they need. Here are the top ten ways to cut the insurance fat and still maintain the right kind of coverage for your financial body type.

CUT HOMEOWNER'S INSURANCE COSTS

Most people have their homeowner's insurance paid as part of the mortgage payment and don't think to get an annual review on this policy. Each year a family should ask their agent how to reduce costs through discounts for nonsmokers, fire prevention devices in the home, security systems, or a new tile roof. Carry only the coverage needed. Most families should carry the Homeowner's Broad form and only up to 90% of the home's value—*don't* include the land in this coverage. You can't collect more than the home value if there is a total loss, so don't pay for additional premiums. Further reduce premiums by increasing the deductible to $500, $1,000, or 1% of the total amount of coverage.

RECONSIDER REPLACEMENT VALUE FOR CONTENTS INSURANCE

There should be *replacement value* on personal property insurance. It only costs a little more, and the additional coverage is worthwhile. For example, if the pipes freeze and permanently damage carpet, replacement value will reimburse the cost of replacing the carpet with the same quality carpet—less the deductible. If there's no replacement value, the carpet will be depreciated, which won't leave much of a check to cover the damages.

PERSONAL ARTICLES RIDERS

If a thief steals jewelry, guns, computer equipment, antiques, coin collections, and other personal items, the homeowner's insurance could cover as little as $1,000 unless they are *itemized*. The cost of this additional coverage depends upon the total amount of the rider.

IDENTITY THEFT PROTECTION

Trying to undo the damage a thief causes when he steals your social security number and ruins your credit could cost thousands of dollars. Protection usually costs about $25 per year and can be added through most homeowner's policies. The following companies offer this coverage: *www.aig.com*; *www.chubb.com*; or *www.farmers.com*.

AUTOMOBILE INSURANCE

Your momma said you should drive the speed limit, and insurance companies agree. Each ticket and each accident add surcharge points and additional premiums to the cost of a policy. Consequently, if you were given a ticket unfairly, it pays to fight it. If another person was at fault in an accident, call the police to the scene to write a police report, which proves there's no fault and removes any surcharge points on the policy. Go for the higher deductibles on comprehensive and collision in order to insure big accidents, not fender benders.

Shop Around

Secure estimates from at least three major companies before purchasing automobile insurance. Reduce the cost of insurance on your car by buying the right kind of car. Some vehicles are far more expensive to insure than others, so check with an insurance agent before buying a car. If possible, use the least expensive car to travel to and from work. "For pleasure only" vehicles have the cheapest rating, so use that on the most expensive vehicle.

Auto Insurance Discounts

Some companies offer discounts to nonsmokers and/or nondrinkers (total abstainers). Other discounts can possibly be included for anti-theft devices, safe drivers, multi-car discounts, drivers between ages thirty and sixty, or driver's education courses. Certain professions, such as the military, are sometimes given special discounts. Other companies offer a discount if you carry your homeowner's insurance with them.

Bonus Tip—Insuring Young Drivers

Carefully consider when a teenager gets his driver's license. Once they have a license, even if they don't have a car to drive, they'll have to be listed somewhere on the policy. If the only cars on the policy are fully covered vehicles (comprehension and collision), it could double the premiums!

The best option is to put a teenager as the principal driver on an older vehicle that only carries the basic package—liability, medical, and uninsured motorists. Consider letting the teen pay a portion (or all) of his insurance premium—it's an extra incentive to drive safely.

BUY TERM RATHER THAN WHOLE LIFE

Life insurance is a supplementary provision for the family—not an investment. See complete analysis on pages 136–137, but it is generally more affordable to buy term and invest the difference rather than purchase permanent insurance. There should be enough insurance to pay off debts with adequate principal for the family to live modestly off the interest. For competitive insurance quotes call Select Quote at 1–800–343–1985 or go to *www.quotesmith.com.*

HEALTH INSURANCE

The best and least expensive medical insurance could be from your employer, especially if they pay your premium. This is usually a group policy that includes dependents, but shop around to make sure you are getting the best rate for your dependents. A good health insurance plan should cover 80% of the medical bills in the event of a major illness. If you lose your job, you *might* be able to maintain your insurance (go to *www.cobrahealth.com* for details).

An excellent online source for insurance comparisons is *www.ehealthinsurance.com.* This site researches the optimum plan for your needs and provides the best price because they offer carrier-direct rates with real-time quotes. They also research health insurance providers and policy rates for dental and life insurance as well.

Go to the library and look at the magazine *Bests' Insurance Reports* to find the latest information on A-rated companies. Some self-employed people use Golden Rule (*www.goldenrule.com*) as an option. Consider raising major medical deductibles to $1,000 and make sure the plan has a no-deductible accident provision. Never buy two policies on one person— you pay twice, but you can't collect twice! Don't cancel an existing policy until a new one is in place or there may be a gap in coverage.

HEALTH SAVINGS ACCOUNTS OR HSA

These are new and could possibly be a great option for you. The U.S. Congress recently passed legislation that makes paying for medical expenses much more affordable for consumers. As of January 1, 2004, the new law provides broad access to Health Savings Accounts, which allow consumers to pay for qualified medical expenses with pre-tax dollars (income-tax free!) and save for retirement on a tax-deferred basis.

Basically, a HSA is a tax-favored saving account that is used in conjunction with a high-deductible HSA-eligible health insurance plan to make health care more affordable and to save for retirement.

• Pre-tax money is deposited each year into an HSA and can be easily withdrawn at any time with no penalty or taxes to pay for qualified medical expenses. Withdrawals can also be made for non-medical purposes, but will be taxed as normal income and are subject to a 10% penalty if done prior to age sixty-five.

- Any HSA funds not used each year remain in the account and earn interest tax-free to supplement medical expenses at any time in the future.
- Like an IRA, the account belongs to you, not your employer. But unlike an IRA, your employer *can* contribute to your HSA.

HSAs can be used to pay for many types of medical expenses—even some that are excluded on health insurance plans. These include:

- Health insurance plan deductibles, co-payments, and co-insurance
- Prescription and over-the-counter drugs
- Dental services, including braces, bridges, and crowns
- Vision care, including glasses and laser eye surgery
- Psychiatric and certain psychological treatments
- Long-term care services
- Medically related transportation and lodging

Typically, HSAs cannot be used to pay health insurance premiums, although there are exceptions for the following:

- Health insurance premiums if you are receiving federal or state unemployment benefits
- Premiums for COBRA qualified health insurance
- Long-term care insurance premiums
- Premiums for a health plan (other than a Medicare supplemental policy for an individual age sixty-five or older)

One important footnote is that you must establish an HSA

before incurring any expenses or the expenses will not qualify.

Not all health insurance plans qualify to be used in conjunction with HSAs, only those that are eligible. This type of insurance plan is often referred to as a High Deductible Health Plan (HDHP) and is typically less expensive than plans with lower deductibles. The following criteria must be met to be considered HSA-eligible:

- The plan must have an annual deductible of at least $1,000 for individuals and at least $2,000 for families.
- The sum of the annual deductible and the other annual out-of-pocket expenses required to be paid under the plan (other than premiums) should not exceed $5,000 for individuals and $10,000 for families.

For a complete list of HSA-eligible plans or to investigate signing up for one of these savings accounts, go to *www.ehealth insurance.com*. Since the funds you put into this account are carried over each year, the worst-case scenario is that you remain healthy and use the HSA very little. In which case you'd have more money in that account, growing tax-free until you are sixty-five years old, and then you could remove it from the account without paying any taxes. Sounds like a win/win deal to me!

CAN'T GET HEALTH INSURANCE?

For those of you who do not have health insurance, are considered "high risk" individuals, or have preexisting conditions, go to a new site called *www.ehealthinsurance.org*, which is designed for you. This site will help you plug into federal, state, and local programs that can help you with your health services and health insurance needs.

EVERYTHING YOU WANTED TO KNOW ABOUT LIFE INSURANCE

Type of Insurance	Advantages	Disadvantages
Level Term	Level payments over specific period, usually 5, 10, 15, or 20 years; may be convertible to a permanent policy	More expensive than ART in early years; less expensive in later years
Whole Life (permanent)	Fixed premiums; cash value you can borrow against; possible dividends; tax-deferred earnings; guaranteed death benefits	Initially higher premium than term insurance; little flexibility in premium payments
Universal Life (permanent)	Flexible premiums; tax-deferred earning on cash value; access funds; different options allow cash buildup or insurance protection	If interest rates fall, low cash value buildup may cause policy to lapse unless you add money
Variable Life (permanent)	Fixed level premiums; guaranteed death benefit; choice of investment options	Premiums start low but rise with each new term; nothing back if you outlive contract

Annual Renewable Term (ART)	Most coverage for the least money; protection in increments of one year; can renew yearly up to specified age (usually seventy); may be convertible to permanent policy	Potentially higher earnings than other cash value policies but also greater risk
Variable Universal Life (permanent)	Similar to variable life but with flexible payments	You select the investment vehicle that generates your cash value growth (stocks, bonds, etc.), so there's greater risk

Debt Dropper #3: Housing Fixer-Uppers

Housing is usually the largest line item on the family budget. And if you're looking to drop some serious debt, you may have to consider downsizing. But before taking such a dramatic approach to budget cutting, give these housing-savvy measures a try.

HOMEOWNER'S CHECKLIST

To get the most out of your home financially, both now and in the future, it's important to keep a close eye on some specific items.

Information, Please: Keep a copy of the following information in your files and in a safety deposit box: property address, legal description, date of purchase, and previous owner. You should also have current addresses and account or policy numbers on the following: real estate agent, closing agent, title company, insurance company and agent, and the mortgage company.

Identity Theft: Your credit rating greatly impacts your ability to trade up on a home in the future. In order to maintain your good credit rating *and* catch possible identity thief, get a regular copy of your credit report. Go to *www.freecreditreport.com* for a free copy.

Inventory: Take an inventory of the valuables in your home and update it on a regular basis. Periodically there may be a need to take photos and upgrade coverage on the insurance policy. Go to *www.ourfamilyplace.com* for suggested inventory pages.

Insurance: As a former insurance agent, I was able to almost double the size of the clientele for the agency I worked for by doing some simple research. I would find out what people were currently paying for their homeowner's policies and help them find a cheaper rate. Most of these policies are paid through the mortgage company's escrow account. You can save a lot by getting a new quote at renewal time each year. To get started, go to *www.freeinsurancequotes.com* or *www.insweb.com*.

Inexpensive Safety: There are some basic (and inexpensive) security measures that every house should be equipped with. They are: dead-bolt locks ($20-$45), motion-detector security lights ($20-$60), window locks ($5-$10), smoke detectors ($8-

$35), carbon monoxide detectors ($35-$75), and fire extinguishers ($20-$60).

Interest Rates: The rule of thumb for a good value on refinancing your home is that you should plan on being in the home for at least another three years, and the *fixed* (not variable) interest rate should be a *minimum* of two full points lower than what you are currently paying. Here's an example of a 30-year term mortgage, originally financed at 9.25% APR and with 23 years remaining on the loan, with a refinance for 15 years at 7.25% APR. The original finance amount was $100,000, and the balance is $93,808.

Original Loan		Refinanced Loan	
Mortgage Amount	$100,000	Mortgage Amount	$93,808
Monthly	$823.00	Monthly	$856.00
Payments Left	276	Payments Left	180
Total of Remaining Payments	$227,148	Total of Remaining Payments	$154,080

Taken from *www.ourfamilyplace.com/homeowner/refinance.html*

Instant HELOCS: A home equity line of credit is similar to your banker selling you a gun and teaching you how to pull the trigger to shoot yourself in the foot. That's what happens when a HELOC credit card is secured. The credit companies tout it as "a convenient way to access your home's equity without refinancing your mortgage every time you need money." Yeah, right.

When they say "convenient," think Burger King convenient.

The credit card promo reads: "Your credit is available 24-hours-a-day for everyday purchases like gas, groceries, and clothes, or whenever you need cash. NowLine can be used at millions of locations worldwide, anywhere Visa is accepted."

Jeanne Sahadi, *CNN/Money*, sums it up this way: "Now, if a family is truly hard up for cash and faced with the awful choice of paying for life's daily expenses by credit card or using a HELOC, one could argue a HELOC is the better option because it's the least expensive in the short term. That's because HELOCs, which are tied to the prime rate, carry lower rates than credit cards and the interest is typically tax-deductible. But for a bank to suggest in its promos that HELOCs are a fine way to pay for dinner? I think that's indecent."

A HELOC credit card should be avoided unless your family is unemployed or on the verge of losing your car or home. It's just another way to borrow on your future in order to live for today. It's also another way to incur more debt, and it will keep you from paying off your home that much sooner.

A home equity line of credit is similar to your banker selling you a gun and teaching you how to pull the trigger to shoot yourself in the foot.

Improvement List: It's important to keep a list of all improvements on your home—from a new air conditioner to a hot water heater. It can help you now (on your taxes) and later (when you sell your home). Also, capital gains taxes will be based on the difference between the sale price (less any selling expenses) minus the adjusted basis. You should check with your tax adviser each year, but the IRS usually defines improvements as those items that "add to the value of your home, prolong its useful life, or adapt it to new uses." Examples include: putting a recreation room in your unfinished basement; adding another bathroom or bedroom; putting up a fence; installing new plumbing or wiring; getting a new roof; or paving your driveway. You can add improvements to the basic value of your property, but be sure to keep meticulous records of these expenses.

Inspections: It can be very alarming and costly to discover that your home has some kind of pest infestation. Not only will you have to pay the expense of debugging your home, there may be the added expense of repairing structural damage. Have a pest-control professional inspect your home on a regular basis.

Involvement in Taxes: When was the last time you even thought of reviewing your real estate taxes. I recently spoke with our local county tax assessor and he said that very few people dispute their tax assessment, but there are times it is important to do so. Unless your situation is an obvious oversight to which the assessor agrees, you will need to be prepared to back up your claim regarding your property value. This could include an appraisal or a comparative market analysis. The comparative market analysis will document recorded sales of houses similar to yours, and these services are sometimes offered free from real estate agents. However, the assessment by a real estate agent is not the legal document provided by a licensed appraiser.

$ $ $

Don't feel that you need to do everything on this list by next week. But if you do just a couple per month, by the year's end you will have a firm grip on making sure that *you* own your home rather than the other way around!

FISCAL FITNESS WORKOUT

House Maintenance Checklist

There's an old saying that an ounce of prevention is worth a pound of cure. There is a lot you can do to prevent unneeded and untimely expenses.

Exterior Items to be checked	MONTHLY	EVERY 3 MONTHS	EVERY 6 MONTHS
Roof: Visually check shingles from ground. Watch for missing shingles or broken pieces. Check gutters and downspouts.			✓
Gutters and downspouts: Check and remove any debris to assure unobstructed water flow away from foundation.			✓
Veneer or siding: With brick, watch for deteriorating bricks or masonry. For siding, watch for warping or rot. Check all painted surfaces.			✓
Windows and doors: Check caulking around doors and windows, glazing around window panes.			✓
Lawn and garden: Watch for accumulation of tree limbs, branches, debris that can attract wood eating insects.		✓	
Asphalt Driveways: Check for cracks or deterioration. Reseal if necessary.			✓
Heating and cooling: Make sure outside unit is unobstructed. Clean unit with garden hose.		✓	

Interior Items to be checked	MONTHLY	EVERY 3 MONTHS	EVERY 6 MONTHS
Attic: Examine for evidence of any leaks.		✓	
Baths: Check for evidence of any leaks, especially around toilets and under sinks (vinyl tile will usually discolor if water is getting underneath it). Check grout on any ceramic tile.	✓		
Kitchen: Check for leaks under sink and around dishwasher. Check burner operation on stove. Check grout on any ceramic tile.	✓		
Kitchen: Clean dust from refrigerator condenser (rear of unit).		✓	
Heating System: Change filter, check coils for buildup.	✓		
Water Heater: Check for signs of leaks.	✓		
Water Heater: Drain to remove any sediment. In areas with hard water, drain every 3 months.			✓
Smoke Detectors: Check operation.	✓		
Smoke Detectors: Change batteries.			✓
Basement or crawl space: Check for cracks or any sign of dampness or leaks. Check for any evidence of termites or wood-eating insects.			✓

(Taken from *www.ourfamilyplace.com/homeowner/maintain.html*)

section three:
FOREVER FREE

CHAPTER NINE

The Personal Trainer Gets Personal

*Getting the Right Kind of Help
When You Need It*

I was on top of the world, or so it seemed from my vantage point. I don't know about you, but there are few things that make me feel as close to heaven as mountains, sunshine, and a cool breeze. Combine that with a Harry & David's chocolate truffle and a cup of coffee, and I can almost hear the angels singing. This lovely interlude happened for me during a Tennessee speaking engagement. I was enjoying an eight-hour furlough as the keynote speaker at Mountain Top Conferences in Pigeon Forge—a beautiful mountain village that possesses two of a woman's favorite things—beauty and shopping. While I was savoring my chocolate from a park bench and looking over my day's booty from the outlet mall, my friend Brenda disappeared into a children's shop.

There I sat on my park bench, in a sleeveless blue-jean Liz Claiborne designer dress ($19.99), wearing trendy Enzo wedgie shoes ($21.99), and bedazzled with gold and silver Premier Design jewelry—free from hosting a party for Brenda's home business. I felt pretty, witty, and wise. And if all of this weren't enough, I got to share my chocolate and plenty of belly laughs with my fellow Bargain Queen and lifelong friend. What a special treat. Yep, nothing could spoil this perfect afternoon.

Or so I thought.

I had just savored my last sip of coffee when I realized Brenda was still out browsing. Too comfy to go traipsing around looking for her, I did what any temporarily friend-deprived shopper would do. I grabbed my cell phone and checked up on another friend miles away from home. Vicki and I exchanged newsy banter about the conference and my bargains. Fellow shoppers continued to stroll by, gracing me with toothy grins. *Hmmm*, I thought. *People sure are friendly. They must be loving this gorgeous weather as much as I am.*

I wrapped up my conversation with Vicki-girl just as Brenda walked out from conquering the Gap for Kids outlet store.

This dear sweet friend smiled broadly at me and said nary a word. Instead, she slowly began to pull something out of her purse. *Oh, how sweet! She's brought me more chocolate.* Alas, no cocoa powder, but a powder compact instead. As she popped the lid to reveal the mirror, she turned it toward me to give me a view of my face.

I expected to see one Chic Chick, an image befitting a keynote speaker. Instead, I saw the face of a thirty-something toddler who had just polished off a chocolate Easter bunny. Somehow I had managed to smear my dark chocolate truffle on my alabaster cheek. In a flash, I understood why so many people had seemed so smiley and friendly when they saw me. (Most embarrassing.)

$ $ $

I figure you've got two choices when you find yourself in an embarrassing situation. You can either cry from the sheer mortification of the moment, or you can have a good laugh, clean yourself up, and live to tell about it. After I stopped laughing, I cleaned the mess off my face and thanked God that Brenda had saved me from further public humiliation. Otherwise, I probably would have been a choco-covered shopper for several more hours, passing by hundreds of shoppers, retailers, and an oblivious cab driver. Dear Brenda. That's what friends are for: They tell you when you're a mess.

There's a Proverb that says, "Two are better than one. Two have a better return for their work than one. If one falls down, the other is there to pick him up, but woe to the man who falls and has no one to pick him up." I call these special people "come alongside friends."

Just as we women have shopping buddies, many of us also have workout buddies. When you're trying to get that body in shape, it helps to know that you have a girlfriend saving a place for you at Pilates class. Sometimes just knowing that your walking partner will be waiting at the edge of her driveway at five-thirty in the morning makes you more motivated to get moving. You're more likely to drag those bones out of bed at five o'clock, throw some cold water on your face, groggily brush your teeth (mothers of preschoolers, be sure you grab the toothpaste and not the Desitin℠), and pull on a pair of comfortable sweats to get out there and meet her.

When it comes to getting your finances in shape, there are times we need a come alongside friend who will play the role of the personal trainer in our life. There might even be an occasion when such a "trainer" will encourage a friend to seek out a financial counselor before they need the financial equivalent of gastric bypass surgery. Of course, this presupposes that you have a sufficient relationship with your friend and care enough about them to take the risk of encouraging them to seek financial help.

What if *you* find yourself in need of a little help to pull you off a financial plateau? One major thing to keep in mind is this: Seeking out the services of a qualified financial counselor is a good thing—it doesn't mean you have failed. It simply means you are smart enough to use the resources available to you in areas where you are not as well trained.

In 2003 about five hundred and fifty-seven thousand people signed up for debt repayment plans and credit-counseling services with Consumer Credit Counseling Service (CCCS) alone. This is according to Lydia Sermons-Ward, a spokesperson for the National Foundation for Credit Counseling (*moneycentral.msn.com*). Of those, says Sermons-Ward, "About half were expected to successfully complete their plans. The other half were expected to drop out, with some of those filing for bankruptcy."

If you are able to pay your bills and are current on your accounts, you almost certainly do not need credit counseling. Generally speaking, you might need counseling if you:

- Can't pay the minimums on all your credit cards
- Are regularly late on paying one or more of your regular bills
- Are being called by creditors and collection agencies
- Cannot seem to be able to work out a repayment plan on your own.

There is a warning you should heed: If you allow your situation to get too bad, you might reach the point where even credit counseling can't help you. Credit card companies can only cut their payments so much to give you enough room to breathe. This is why you need to know when to go for help.

"Do I Need a Financial Advisor?" Quiz

Here's a quick quiz to see if you are a candidate for a financial "personal trainer." It will require a little research on your part as you look back on your answers from other parts of this book—but it will be worth it to know if you could truly benefit from professional assistance.

1. Did you score 18 or less on the chapter 1 quiz?
2. Are you a "high-debt-risk" money personality—an Entrepreneur, High Roller, Hunter, or Producer from chapter 2?
3. Do you operate in a "high-debt-risk" money style of an Avoider or Overspender from chapter 2?
4. Did you score low in satisfaction in chapter 3's "Fiscal Fitness Workout: Money Attitude Quiz"?
5. Does your debt pattern more closely resemble that of the beast rather than Beauty (chapter 4)?
6. Are you unwilling, or feel you are unable, to take the "Giving Challenge" from chapter 5?
7. Are your overall credit-to-debt ratios of one to two (50%) or greater? (See chapter 6 and remember, the larger the fraction, the worse for your FICO score.)
8. Go to *www.crown.org* or *www.consumercredit.com* for

a "Credit Card Minimum Payment" tool, and crunch the numbers for a "minimum-payment" plan on your consumer debt (not mortgage debt). Will it take you ten years or more to pay your debt if you pay only the minimum?

9. Have you tried, unsuccessfully, on your own, to get out of debt and gain control of your finances for three or more years?

10. Have you ever consolidated five or more loans, taken out a home equity loan, or filed bankruptcy in order to eliminate credit card debt?

Just as it is easier to lose ten pounds rather than one hundred, it is also easier to lose a little debt rather than a lot.

If you answered yes to three or more of these questions, you are a candidate for professional financial assistance. You might only be on the cusp of a significant debt problem, but why not find help sooner than later? Just as it is easier to lose ten pounds rather than one hundred, it is also easier to lose a little debt rather than a lot. Plus, you gain the ability to learn how to "eat right and exercise," to manage your money, and save for the future.

But how do you find the right counselor to fit your needs?

Randy was deeply in debt and desperate. He had seen all the television and Internet ads from credit counseling services that promised to help him. He was also approached by a company that assured him it could painlessly make his debts go away. "Is this," he inquired via an e-mail, "too good to be true?" Often the answer is yes.

Randy was thinking of entering a world that is "fraught with fraud, misrepresentation, and controversy," according to Liz Pulliam Weston, financial expert and staff writer with Moneycentral.msn.com. "Debt counseling," says Weston, "has become a $7 billion industry, but not all the players are legitimate. The best credit counseling can help people who are behind on their debts get back on their feet. Fly-by-night outfits can disappear with your money, and what remains of your credit rating. In between the two are a whole fleet of operators who may or may not leave you better off than you are now."

Just as recently as a decade ago this industry was dominated by the National Foundation for Credit Counseling, whose non-profit affiliate was Consumer Credit Counseling Services. Their specialty was (and is) negotiating lower interest rates, creating payment plans, and developing a budget for people who had financial problems. Weston says, "Today, you can find the Consumer Credit Counseling Service in just about any city."

A rise in consumer debt in the 1990s helped create hundreds of for-profit rivals to the CCCS. Many have million-dollar advertising budgets, highly developed Internet campaigns, and legitimate-sounding names. Some of these organizations are solid and do a good job of helping consumers pay off their debt. Others require hefty up-front fees and pay their executives and marketing departments huge salaries funded by your debt problems. It's far better to put that money toward paying off your debt rather than seeing it go toward some fat cat's salary. These unethical businesses are beginning to target customers who don't even have significant debt problems but are unhappy with the current interest rates they are paying. You don't need these guys for something that simple. Just make the phone call and ask the credit card company to lower the APR—an amazing number of customer service representatives are authorized to lower APRs over the phone.

According to Weston, the situation gets worse than that. "The worst aren't credit counselors at all. Usually billing themselves as specialists in 'debt settlement,' they promise to help you get rid of your debts for pennies on the dollar—after you've paid an up-front fee that can be $3,000 or more. Typically, by the time I hear about these companies, they've already absconded with people's cash, disconnected their phones, and set up shop somewhere new with a different name."

So how do you know if a financial planning agency is legitimate?

Top Ten Questions to Ask a Prospective Financial Advisor

If you don't have a local office of the CCCS, you will need to find a local financial advisor. Here are the top ten questions to ask when choosing a financial planner, according to the Certified Financial Planner Board of Standards, Inc., or CFP®:

1. What experience do you have?

- How long has the planner been in practice?
- What are the number and types of companies with which she has been associated?
- What is her work experience, and how does it relate to her current practice?

- Select a financial planner who has experience counseling individuals on their financial needs.

2. What are your qualifications?

- The term *financial planner* is used (and abused) by many financial professionals. Ask the planner what qualifies him to offer financial planning advice.
- Is he a CFP (Certified Financial Planner™), a Certified Public Accountant-Personal Financial Consultant (CPA-PFC), or a Chartered Financial Consultant (ChFC)?
- If the planner holds one of these designations or certifications, check on his background with the CFP Board or other relevant professional organizations.

3. What services do you offer?

- The services a financial planner offers depends on her credentials, licenses, and areas of expertise.
- Generally planners cannot sell insurance or securities products such as mutual funds or stocks without the proper licenses or give investment advice unless registered with state or federal authorities.
- Some planners offer financial planning advice on a range of topics but do not sell financial products.
- Others may provide advice only in specific areas, such as estate planning or on tax matters.

4. What is your approach to financial planning?

- What type of clients and financial situations does she typically like to worth with?

- Some prefer to develop one plan by bringing together all your financial goals.
- Others provide advice on specific areas, as needed.
- Find out if the planner will carry out the financial recommendations developed for you or refer you to others who will do so.

5. Will you be the only person working with me?

- The financial planner may work with you or have others assist you.
- If you will be working with others as well, then ask to meet with everyone who will be working with you.
- If the planner works with professionals outside his practice (such as attorneys, insurance agents, or tax specialists), get a list of their names to check on their backgrounds.

6. How will I pay for your services?

- Ask the planner to tell you clearly (in writing) how she will be paid for the services provided. There are several ways planners could be paid.

  Salary—They may be paid by the company for which they work. Their employer bills you and they pay the planner's salary.

  Fees—They may charge an hourly rate, a flat rate, or a percentage of your assets and/or income.

  Commissions—These would be paid by a third party from the products sold to you to carry out the financial planning recommendations.

Combination—Sometimes there is a combination of fees and commissions.

7. How much do you typically charge?

- The financial planner should be able to provide you with an estimate of possible costs based on the work to be performed.
- Costs would include the planner's hourly rates or flat fees or the percentage he would receive as a commission on products you purchase.

8. Could anyone besides me benefit from your recommendations?

- Some business relationships or partnerships that a planner has could affect her professional judgment while working with you, *inhibiting the planner from acting in your best interests*.
- Ask the planner to provide you with a description of any conflicts of interest in writing.
- The planner may also have relationships or partnerships that should be disclosed to you, such as business she receives for referring you to an insurance agent, accountant, or attorney.

9. Have you ever been publicly disciplined for any unlawful or unethical actions in your professional career?

- Several government and professional regulatory organizations, such as the National Association of Securities Dealers (NASD), your state insurance and securities departments, and CFP Board keep records on the disciplinary action for these individuals.

• Ask what organizations the planner is regulated by and conduct a background check.

10. Can I have it in writing?

• Ask the planner to provide you with a written agreement that details the services that will be provided.
• Keep this document in your files for future reference.

If a planner will not comply with your requests or refuses to answer any of these questions, you've just found one planner you will *not* want to work with!

CHECK

To check the disciplinary history of a Financial Planner or Advisor go to:

Certified Financial Planner Board of Standards, Inc.
888–237–6275 or *www.CFP.net*
North American Securities Administrators Association
202–737–0900 or *www.nasaa.org*
National Association of Insurance Commissioners
816–842–3600 or *www.naic.org*
National Association of Securities Dealers Regulation
800–289–9999 or *www.nasdr.com*
National Fraud Exchange (fee involved)
800–822–0416
Securities and Exchange Commission
202–942–7040 or *www.sec.gov*

FIND

To find a Financial Planner or Advisor in your area go to:

Financial Planning Association
    800–282–7526 or *www.fpanet.org*
National Association of Personal Financial Advisors
    888–333–6659 or *www.napfa.org*
American Institute of Certified Public Accountants-Personal Financial Planning Division
    888–999–9256 or *www.aicpa.org*
Society of Financial Service Professionals
    888–243–2258 or *www.financialpro.org*

RED FLAGS TO WATCH FOR

If at any time any of the following occur, this should be a red flag in working with someone in the area of credit counseling or financial planning:

- **Big upfront fees.** The Consumer Credit Counseling Services typically charge a $10 setup fee. If you're paying a lot more than this (unless you require additional services that justify a higher fee), then you may be the one who is getting set up.

- **No accreditation.** Legitimate credit counseling firms are associated with one of the organizations mentioned earlier. Check to make sure the person you're working with is accredited.

- **Delayed or missing payments.** Some companies take your first month's payments as a fee, rather than passing the money to your creditors. Missing payments can hurt your FICO score. Find out, up front, how much of each monthly payment is going to your creditors and when it will be sent to them.

- **Promises, promises.** If it sounds too good to be true—it usually is. Beware of hasty promises to settle your debts for little or no money, without hurting your credit rating. These companies may help you pay back what you owe at lower interest rates, but most acknowledge that there may be some effect on your credit rating and ability to obtain new credit.

EFFECT ON YOUR CREDIT

Some people do not want to go to a financial counselor because they believe it will trash their credit score or be "worse than bankruptcy." This isn't true. It may or may not have an impact on your credit. It may be true that some lenders may not want to do business with you after you've completed your plan, but others will.

In contrast, a bankruptcy, which is looked upon by all mainstream creditors as a huge blight on your credit report, is worse. These lenders, who want to have customers with good credit, typically will not do business with you for the decade that the bankruptcy remains on your record.

Some agencies will renegotiate lower interest rates and the lender—such as First USA, the credit card giant—will require three payments at the lower rate before they remove the delinquency mark on your report. Being reported as late or delinquent can hurt your FICO score, so you need to address these issues early on in your discussions with your counselor.

There are those creditors who will not work with someone who is signed up in credit counseling programs. On the other hand, some creditors view the credit counselor's involvement as a sign that that person is getting their credit under control.

$ $ $

I learned a long time ago that there aren't any easy answers when you find yourself in a public place with chocolate on your face, and I was reminded of it in that Tennessee mountain paradise I described at the beginning of this chapter. The same is true of financially "having chocolate on your face." But by allowing your situation to go from bad to worse, you'll find it that much harder to clean up when you can no longer avoid it in the long run. If you're in this situation, please deal with it ASAP. You'll be glad you did.

CHAPTER TEN

Raising Fiscally Fit Kids

Ten Things Your Child Should Know
About Money

The bride wore white.

She couldn't stop smiling.

The groom wore a yarmulke.

He couldn't stop laughing.

The father of the bride wore black.

He couldn't stop crying.

We were launching the oldest of our seven children into the adult world of marriage, and it was a day that every girl looks forward to and every little girl's father dreads. We want our children to grow up and make wise choices, and Missy had done that—but how did this day arrive *so soon*?

Wasn't it just yesterday that my Beloved had introduced me to my stepdaughters for the first time? Nervous as I was, Missy and Mandy had turned out to be two beautiful, and smart, little girls, and now Missy Kay was becoming Melissa Rosenblit, and all we did was blink our eyes and move around the country a few times.

Her intended, Moran, is God's perfect choice for Missy. They courted smart, planned the wedding smart, and married smart. In fact, their first kiss on the lips occurred after the Messianic rabbi said, "You may kiss the bride." How's that for a radical departure from the norm? But they have no regrets.

They're also a fiscally fit couple, learning to live below their means while pursuing their mutual dreams. Missy took a year off midway through college to earn money for her education so that when she returned to (and graduated from) Columbia University, she could do so with minimal debt. She earned scholarships, was part of a work-study program, and made minimal use of student loans. Her smart move meant fewer bills when she got married.

So our Missy is money smart *and* she married smart. What else could a parent ask for?

Only one thing.

A grandbaby.

But that will have to wait . . . or so they say.

One down, six more to go.

$ $ $

Statistics say there is a better chance that today's newly married couples *won't* make it in their new married life than that they will. But there are certain things they can do to tip the scales in their favor. What's the No. 1 thing parents can do to launch their kids well and to help them maximize their chances for success? What is the No. 1 concept parents can teach their children in order to help them succeed in relationships and in marriage? Let's look at some possible answers to that question.

Communication? When I wrote the book *The New Bride Guide*, I included a list of all the areas that a good premarital counselor will explore. One of the top areas is communication, and while that's important, it's not the reason most marriages fail.

Fidelity? We want to teach our kids the importance of integrity, truthfulness, and faithfulness in relationships, and the lack of these characteristics has been the death knell of many a marriage. But adultery isn't the primary reason marriages fail.

Faith? Well, then, it must be faith, right? If we train our kids to have a strong faith in God, then they will surely have an advantage in marriage, correct? We've all heard the saying "The couple that prays together, stays together." Unfortunately, the stark statistic is that just as many marriages of Christian (or religious) couples fail as those who do not have a strong faith—the statistics inside the church are identical to those outside the church.

Am I saying that teaching our kids how to communicate, have integrity in their lives, and develop a strong spiritual life is all in vain? Absolutely not. I'm only saying that parents spend the majority of their time teaching their kids about everything but the *real* reason most marriages fail. So I'm about to make a radical statement based on the simple fact that the No. 1 reason cited in divorce is "arguments over money issues" (*www.aba.com*).

So here it is, my **Radical Statement**: *If you want to help your kids succeed in their future marriage, make sure they are fiscally fit by the time they're grown.*

Teach them all the other values of life too—but make sure they know about money. Here are the things your child should have mastered by the time they're launched.

Top Ten Financial Values for Every Child

- *The Value of a Good Work Ethic*
- *The Value of a Dollar*
- *The Value of Budgeting*
- *The Value of Saving and Not Spending*
- *The Value of Investing*
- *The Value of Delayed Gratification*
- *The Value of Sharing*
- *The Value of Diligence*
- *The Value of Responsibility and Accountability*
- *The Value of Rest*

Some of these may not seem like financial values, but as you read on you'll see how these values all contribute to helping an individual develop good money sense. It is extremely important to realize we don't have cookie-cutter kids—they are all different and uniquely gifted. I may have been able to balance my own checkbook at twelve, but my daughter may not master this until she's fifteen. One of your children may be able to make a bed perfectly by the time they're four, and another may not be physically able to do the same chore until they are eight or nine. It's not that one child is smarter or better behaved than the other, they are just operating on different timetables. So use the following information as a guideline, but let each child progress at his or her own pace.

Let's look at them in greater detail for all age groups: "Youngsters" (ages 2 to 6), "Middlers" (ages 7 to 12), and "Teens" (ages 13 to 18).

If you want to help your kids succeed in their future marriage, make sure they are fiscally fit by the time they're grown.

THE VALUE OF A GOOD WORK ETHIC

Defined: *The ability to know how to work hard and find pleasure in a job well done.*

Youngsters: Younger children begin to learn a work ethic through routine and through helping their parents. A child on a schedule learns that there is a time and place for everything and this structure is the beginning of financial readiness.

With a lot of help and positive reinforcement, little ones can learn to pick up their toys. For example, when Philip was little, I'd say, "Let's pick up your toys!" and act excited and clap my hands. When he would manage to get a block into the toy box, I'd say, "Philip helps! Yes, that's a good job." Notice I did not say, "Good boy!" Never praise the child for the work he's done, but praise the work. Your son isn't a "good boy" because he does work, he's a good boy because he's yours and you love him unconditionally. He does a "good job" when he's working.

Conversely, you should never put a negative spin on *the child*, only *the action*. He isn't a bad boy because he didn't pick up his toys. He may have done a poor job at the task, but never verbally attack a child's psyche or personhood when it comes to work failures. They will learn to dislike work if that is your approach.

Let your child help rake and pick up leaves, gather donations for the Salvation Army, and even cook in the kitchen (being mindful of safety issues with small children). When Jonathan and Joshua were two and four, they helped me bake hundreds of cookies for the "Airman Cookie Drive." I gave them the "job" of rolling the snickerdoodle cookie dough in a bag of cinnamon sugar. They wore their little aprons and washed their chubby hands for the job. It was only after we'd baked about one hundred cookies that I realized that each time they'd put a ball in the sugar bag—they'd take a tiny bite out of the dough first. Not surprisingly, they each had quite a tummy-ache that night (which reinforces why most jobs with toddlers and preschoolers require extra supervision)!

Middlers: This is the age where you can introduce the concept of "Do all your work cheerfully." The first time your child begins to grumble over having to fold a load of laundry (or other job) you can institute the following:

In our family, we are committed to helping you learn how to do a job well without grumbling or complaining. This will help you later in life. We are so committed to helping you learn this that if you complain when we give you work, you will automatically do twice the work until you learn to do it without complaining.

So when I ask Daniel to take out the trash, and he grouses, "Why do I always have to do this; why doesn't Philip help?" Then he takes out the trash *and vacuums the stairs*. Or when Joshua is asked to fold a load of laundry and stomps down the hall, throwing a hissy fit—he folds *two loads* of laundry.

All we have to say is "Do I hear you complaining?" to get a response of "Oh no, Mama! We're not complaining. I'll get to that laundry right away." This technique may not work for all children in all families—but it's worked on our five children at home.

Teens: Once each of our teens hit that special number (thirteen) they suddenly became an independent, emancipated person, full of self-knowledge and special rights. One of those inalienable rights they'd like to assume is the "pursuit of happiness" coupled with "the freedom from chores." Almost instantaneously it seemed, they were above the concept of manual labor, and it was easier to peel a grape than to get them to hold down their part of the family workload.

Yet it is precisely during this critical time that they need us to hold them accountable for work. Otherwise, they could develop poor work ethic characteristics that would impact their grades, ability to complete projects, and eventually their employability as an adult. The "twice the work" factor is in full effect in our home with three teens. The emotional fortitude required to follow through on work ethic principles oftentimes has me begging for a trip to Bora Bora—definitely *without* kids. But the good news is, I rarely have to fold laundry at my house.

Another factor that comes into play during these years is whether and how to allow outside work for teens. It's important to make sure they have a safe environment and that you know and trust those people for whom your child works. It's also important that they learn to do their jobs well and with a good attitude. Daniel worked at Dairy Queen during the summer of his fifteenth year and was promoted to shift manager by the next summer. This experience did three things for him: (1) It helped him save enough to pay for a portion of his truck; (2) it helped him learn how to be a good follower as well as an effective leader; and (3) it taught him that he *really* wants to get a college degree so he doesn't have to work in a fast-food place to support his family.

Philip is now working part-time to earn money for a portion of his car and is learning the same principles. There are plenty of days when he'd rather sleep in on a day off from school than do odd jobs at our neighbor's trucking company—but the reminder that he won't have a car keeps him going. It also teaches him to be a self-starter with a solid work ethic.

THE VALUE OF A DOLLAR

Defined: *The ability to know how much work power is required for the purchase of goods or services.*

Youngsters: When your little one sees you get money from the ATM, they begin to think that it grows there (instead of on trees). It's important to begin to train them early that "Mama earned this money, and I take it out of my account when I need it." Or, "Daddy put this money in the bank, and now I take it out to buy things for our family—but I worked for this money." They may be far too young to fully appreciate the value of those dollars at this age, but once again you are laying the foundation for financial principles that will be taught (and caught) at a later time.

Another good teaching experience can happen when you go to the store with your child. It's all right to say, "Mommy has to work six hours at her job at the bank in order to earn the money to buy these groceries." You don't have to do this each time (it would be overkill) but occasionally this not only reinforces a work ethic but it also begins to associate the exchange of labor hours for goods and services.

Middlers: By the time your child is in this age group, you can slowly begin to introduce the idea of how long it takes them, in allowance money, to earn enough to pay for an item they want. For example, they may say, "I want the *Pirates of the Caribbean* video game; it's really cool!" You need to respond, "How many weeks' allowance will that game cost you?" When they begin to look at items in light of the hours they have to work to pay for it, they begin to learn the value of a dollar.

Teens: This is the age where they should naturally be equating recreational activities with hours worked. They could have one day at Six Flags that would cost them three weeks' work at their part-time job. It's also a good age to begin to talk to them about some of your household expenses and obligations so that they can gain a greater appreciation of the value of a dollar. For example, you could tell them about depreciation on a vehicle once you purchase it or the total amount of interest paid for a seven-year car loan (and the end value of the car).

THE VALUE OF BUDGETING

Defined: *The ability to develop, tweak, and stay on a budget in order to meet financial objectives.*

Youngsters: They can begin to have "fun" budgets, where you go to a department store and let them spend a dollar. Guide them and coach them in their decisions and also use the opportunity to teach them about sales tax. You can also let this age group have their own budget for Christmas—but only at the dollar store. This teaches them to think through their selections and work hard to get the most for their limited budget.

Middlers: The fun budgets continue at this age, but can begin to include trips to restaurants. Estimate what it will cost to buy their dinner and add a bit of a pad to that amount. You will give your child the amount for dinner as their "budget" (they never spend their own money on a family outing). Be sure they know that they can keep what they don't spend. If they want to forgo dessert or drink water instead of soda, then they can pocket the difference.

This type of approach can also include fun budgets on trips to the zoo, a theme park, or for souvenirs on vacation. One final area that older middlers can budget is for school supplies. The parents will give their child the money and put them on a budget per semester. Let them manage the purchase of initial supplies as well as ongoing school necessities. It's amazing how your child will no longer "lose" paper and pens when it's their "own" money that will pay for those additional expenses.

Teens: By this age, they should be managing all the aforementioned budgets plus their own clothing budget. They will also be paying for most of their recreational expenses—outside of family outings. A teen should never have to pay their own way to a restaurant, amusement park, or movie when he attends with his family. However, when he goes out with friends, he needs to be aware of the fact that this will come out of his budget.

It's wise to have a regular budget meeting with your teen

once a month to help them tweak their budgets. You might need to remind them there is a prom coming up (recreation budget) or that winter is just around the corner and they'll need a heavy coat (clothing budget).

THE VALUE OF SAVING AND NOT SPENDING

Defined: *The ability to find the best value on goods and services wanted or needed.*

Youngsters: This group can begin to learn how to "save" money by using coupons and shopping sales. I used to give my little guys a coupon for a candy bar and then the money to pay for it. When the checker said, "That will be eighty-nine cents," they could then hand over their coupon and get the item for pennies or for free.

Middlers: By this age they are ready to do comparison shopping. If they want to save for a bike, CD player, video game, or other "big" item, take them to *www.froogle.com* in order to research the price on the item. Print out the best price and take it to the mall to compare with the department store prices. Each time they save money, encourage this by praising them for their efforts. Be sure to brag on them within hearing distance to other family members and friends.

Teens: Teach your teen how to "conquer a store." Walk them through the sale racks and point out how a similar shirt or pair of shoes costs substantially more at full price. If they are on their own clothing budget, they are going to be more likely to learn how to get more for less money. You might even want to take them into your insurance agent's office and let her explain the difference in price for a youthful driver who has tickets and one who is a good driver. This teaches them that sometimes "saving" money is a result of good behavior and responsible living.

THE VALUE OF INVESTING

Defined: *The ability to realize that my financial future will not take care of itself; I must take care of it through the miracle of compounding interest.*

Youngsters: Young children can learn that the money they put in a banking account will one day earn them interest. While they are still too young to open their own savings account, they're not too young for you to begin to explain to them how accounts work when you go to the bank.

For example, the next time you and your four-year-old go to the bank to make a deposit, tell her, "When I put my money in this bank, I earn more money through interest. When you are seven or eight years old, we will open your own account in this bank."

Middlers: This is the age to open their first savings account, depending upon the maturity of the child. It's important to require that your child save at least 10% of their allowance each week. About once a month, allow them to go to the bank with you to make their own deposits. You might even check with your local bank to see if they have a child-friendly savings account, such as a "Looney Tunes" account, in order to make saving money fun.

When Daniel was six years old, we had a bank that would give a child their choice of a plastic dinosaur for every ten dollars they deposited in a one-month period. Daniel loved prehistoric creatures and was committed to saving a good part of his allowance and even part of his birthday money.

Teens: Depending upon the maturity of your teen, they should have a substantial savings account that would allow them to open their first mutual fund. There are junior funds that can be opened with as little as $200 to $300 and only require a monthly contribution of $25 to $50. Go to our previous chapter on savings and show your teen the miracle of compounding interest.

You might want to establish a "contract labor" clause with your teen to help them make their minimum payment. For example, Daniel is contracted to baby-sit his siblings whenever we need him, and he gets $50 for the month. Some months he may only sit for five hours, thus making $10 per hour. But other months he may sit for 20 hours, only making $2.50 an hour. We established a yard-work contract with Philip for mowing in the summer, raking in the fall, shoveling in the winter, and spring-cleaning in the spring. Try coming up with a creative approach that will work for your child.

The Value of Delayed Gratification

Defined: *The ability to understand that sometimes the best things in life are those you have to wait for.*

Youngsters: This is the "Wally World Syndrome" time. You now see the meltdowns that occur when a demanding toddler or preschooler holds mom hostage for a $7.99 Nerf Gun. This is the age to nip that in the bud, and we've done it with all of our five children at home—it works! You draw the boundaries in the parking lot: "Mom isn't going to buy you anything in there today, and if you act ugly about it, then I'm going to take you home and you won't get to watch *SpongeBob SquarePants* this afternoon."

As soon as sweetie child turns into a spoiled banana baby in the store, you must follow through on those boundaries you established, by leaving your cart in the store, taking them to the parking lot, and getting into your car and driving home. You will only have to do this once or twice to completely break them of this syndrome.

On the other hand, if you do not nip this in the bud, your child will learn how to manipulate you for what they want as they grow up, and they will not learn the value of delayed gratification.

Middlers: When your child wants to buy something in the store with their savings or allowance, play the "three-day wait" game in order to teach them this value. Tell them they can buy it in three days, and then mark it in your PalmPilot that you need to come back to the store at that time. You'll be amazed at how many times the child has changed his mind and no longer wants the item. Use this as a teachable moment to explain the idea of impulse buying and the value of delayed gratification.

Teens: This value is going to prepare your teen for a life of financial freedom rather than bondage to debt. It is also going to come in handy when their peer group tempts them to sample drugs or take an offer from a promiscuous classmate. So often financial skills are just plain character issues that manifest themselves in similar ways.

If your child has a prepaid credit card in their pocket, they will also have the opportunity to learn delayed gratification and victory over the temptation of plastic. These cards are paid for by the teen's savings account and are limited by the amount they've paid into the card. They are somewhat like a debit card for savings, but they look and feel just like a regular credit card.

Monitor your teen's spending patterns by viewing the monthly statements with them. Since they know that you are going to do this each month, this accountability will make them more mindful of delaying purchases until they are sure the item is a good value and not just an impulse buy. Establish a boundary with them. If they spend to the point where their card is below 50% funded in any given month (they spend $125 of a $250 card), then they will no longer have the privilege of carrying the card with them.

It's far better for your child to fail in some of these areas while they are in your home, rather than pay the price of a more permanent and impacting blight on their credit report when they are in college.

The Value of Sharing

Defined: *The ability to hold my material possessions, time, and financial resources with open hands rather than a closed fist.*

Youngsters: Let your child help you gather groceries, clothing, and toys for a nonprofit thrift shop, Veteran's Home, homeless shelter, the Salvation Army, or Goodwill. Talk to them about the importance of sharing with others as you deliver these goods to the donation point.

Middlers: Adopt a third-world child as a family project and put your child in charge of writing letters to this new friend around the world. Talk about the fact that sponsorship makes the difference between a child living or dying in some cases and it certainly makes the difference between whether they will be educated or not. For more information on this, go to the next chapter.

Teens: At this point your teen should be physically involved in the "sharing" process in a greater way. Make sure they understand that there are a lot of different ways to share: money, possessions, and time. Encourage them to actively be involved in a different approach to sharing each semester. They could volunteer as a soccer coach one season, plan to take a mission trip to build houses in Mexico another season, and raise money for a homeless shelter during another season. There's no limit to how your teen can learn to share if you will lead and empower them to push the limits of generosity.

The Value of Diligence

Defined: *The ability to follow through with a vision for excellence until the job is done.*

Youngsters: Begin to teach your children to finish their work whether it's picking up their toys, clearing the dining room table properly, or taking the laundry basket all the way to the laundry room. It's important that you train them to finish the job even at an early age. This also means that you do not go back and remake their bed after they've done it. It's important to allow them to work at the level in which they can succeed. So if they are learning to make their bed, don't expect them to be an expert in three months.

Middlers: This is the point where you really bear down in teaching your child to finish what they start. If they beg you to take ballet, there should be an agreement on how long they will take the lessons. If the agreement is for a year, then they should take the lessons for a year whether they change their mind midstream or not. If they are a pianist, then they need to make it to that first recital. A good family motto to adopt is: We will finish what we start.

Teens: Teens find it increasingly difficult to finish what they start because of the greater amount of emotion they feel over each and every event in their lives. That's why it's so important to instill this value before they reach the teen years. Mark absolutely clear boundary lines, and they will understand that if they are going to play the saxophone their freshman year, then they are going to play it the entire year. Then you are likely to set them up for success in the diligence department.

THE VALUE OF RESPONSIBILITY AND ACCOUNTABILITY

Defined: *Realizing that I am 100% responsible for my 50% of the partnership with others.*

Youngsters: This is where our own basic attitude toward discipline may need to be examined. Is your yes really a yes? Does your no mean no? If *you* don't know, then how will your child know? The greatest way to teach your child responsibility and accountability is to teach them that *lack* of responsibility has unpleasant consequences. If she doesn't make her bed, then she's going to pay her sister to make it—from her allowance. This seems to be especially important in the formative youngster years. The patterns you set in consistency and follow-through early on will have a lifelong impact on your child.

Middlers: In these years, your elementary-age children should be learning that if they do not follow through on their schoolwork responsibilities, their grades are going to suffer. You can help your child get organized, but there comes a point where you let reality be the best teacher—and you're there at the outcome to coach them, even if they fail.

For example, if your child has a major project due in his class—and he procrastinates until the ninth hour—you aren't required to rush out and buy him the materials he needs in order to complete the project. Allowing him to fail while in his elementary school years can teach him a much needed sense of responsibility and accountability before he reaches high school, when procrastination can really impact his scholarship grades. Admittedly it's tough finding the balance between reminding them of their work and letting them take responsibility for the outcome if they don't. But again, allowing unpleasant consequences to happen can be a valuable teaching tool. (Though it sometimes seems harder on the parent than on the child!)

Teens: If you've suffered through the above process, by the time your child is a teen, it should make those teen years much easier. But it's never too late, and better late than never. There may be no more significant reality lesson that you teach your teen than that there are consequences for our behaviors and attitudes.

This means that when they forget to fill their tank with gas, then they will run out. It also means that if they speed, they might get a ticket. We don't pay for their gas, and we don't fight their tickets. Instead, we allow reality to be the best teacher, and we use these moments as opportunities to teach the values of responsibility and accountability.

> *There may be no more significant reality lesson that you teach your teen than that there are consequences for our behaviors and attitudes.*

The Value of Rest

Defined: *The ability to regroup and recharge without guilt.*

Youngsters: Did you know that having a regular schedule for your child can be the beginning of teaching them financial principles? If there is structure and order in a young child's life, they begin to learn how to structure and order all areas of their lives.

It's important to schedule a nap time in your young child's life, but it's also important for them to learn how to sit quietly in their bedroom and read a book when they've outgrown nap time. Learning to be quiet and comfortable with himself is an acquired skill that you can begin to train your child in by allowing him the benefit of a regular schedule with rest built into that pattern. The next paragraph explains how this works in his financial future.

Middlers: If your children see that you can take a day off or that you have a regular vacation, they'll grow up to do the same in their lives. But if you find it hard to lighten up, spend free time with your family, and learn the value of rest, your child is more likely to follow a workaholic pattern than a pattern of balance.

Middlers need to learn to look forward to their time off as a well-earned rest or break. Something as simple as teaching them to follow through on a task with diligence and then to reward themselves with recreation afterward is a way to instill in them the value of rest.

Teens: It's sometimes hard to persuade your teen to slow down enough for rest. But teenagers sometimes require more rest just to accommodate the physical growth and demands of their busy lives. Some teens need as much sleep as they did when they were toddlers in order to give their bodies the adequate amount of rest to remain healthy.

It is critical during the teen years that you take your teen on vacations with your family—even if it's a camping trip or a visit to an amusement park. Remember that these are the last few years you have with your child as a child. Prioritizing rest and recreational time with them is one of the last investments you'll make in their lives while they're still under your roof and in your care.

You won't regret the additional amount of time you spent with your child while they were growing up, but you will regret those lost weeks and months when you made the decision to overwork instead of taking time to rest, relax, and reconnect.

FISCAL FITNESS WORKOUT

Fiscal Report Card

The following is a report card to grade yourself on your fiscal fitness as a parent. Grade yourself at each age level of your child. By the time they are eighteen, they should have mastered everything on this list. This exercise also gives you the insight into areas that may be weak and need to be strengthened and those areas that are already strong and need to be positively reinforced. Give yourself an E for excellent, S for Satisfactory, or N for Needs Improvement.

Youngsters   **Grade:**
   Ages 2 to 4

- Picks up toys cheerfully   _____
- Obeys parents most of the time   _____
- Is on a schedule for sleep, play, and work
  (or school)   _____

   Ages 4 to 6

- Makes bed in a basic way (not necessarily neat)   _____
- Picks up room regularly   _____
- Brings clothes to hamper   _____
- Knows how to set and clear the table   _____

- Hangs up clothes and puts them in drawers _____
- Knows how to take out the trash _____
- Gives away clothing or toys or money to those in need _____
- Does work without grumbling _____
- Does not throw "Wally World" tantrums _____

Middlers   Grade:

Ages 7 to 10

- Is a master bed maker _____
- Knows how to sort laundry into whites, colors, and darks _____
- Can fold laundry and put it in everyone's room _____
- Is given an allowance _____
- Has a savings account at home and at a bank _____
- Regularly "tithes" from their earnings _____
- Can load and clear the dishwasher _____
- Knows how to vacuum and dust _____
- Manages a fun kid budget (restaurant, zoo, amusement park, etc.) _____

Ages 11 to 12

- Has advanced to "potty training" (they know how to clean a bathroom) _____
- Begins to do additional "jobs" for hire within the home and occasionally for friends or family _____
- Has a savings account with at least $200 to $250 in it _____

- Manages more advanced budgets, such as a
  semester-long school supply budget   _____
- Is learning the meaning of delayed gratification   _____
- Can save up for half of a larger-ticket item they
  want (bike, skates, video game, etc.)   _____
- Can tell you how many hours it takes to work or
  save for goods and services   _____
- Knows how to read a savings account statement   _____
- Is *regularly* contributing to a community
  organization either through volunteer hours or
  donating goods (clothing, toys, money)   _____

Teens   Grade:

Ages 13 to 15

- Is regularly sponsoring a third-world child
  or mission   _____
- Can manage and balance their own checkbook with supervision   _____
- Has enough in savings to take out $200 to $300
  to start a mutual fund   _____
- Is able to do outside jobs for hire among approved
  "employers" in the neighborhood and regular
  summer jobs (appropriate to age and ability)   _____
- Realizes they will continue to do "twice the work"
  if they do not work with a good attitude   _____
- Regularly pays half on larger-ticket items   _____
- Regularly pays for *non-family* outings (movies, theme
  parks, virtual game centers, restaurants, etc.)   _____
- Is saving for a vehicle   _____

- Is aware of the fact their grades in high school will impact their ability to get into college and earn scholarships for college _____
- Understands their primary job in school is to work hard and get the best grades they are capable of making _____

Ages 16 to 18

- Has opened a mutual fund and is contributing monthly to the fund _____
- Can tell you how much money they will earn in their mutual fund by the time they are 45, 55, and 65 if they continue to contribute the minimal amount they are now contributing _____
- Can balance a checkbook without supervision _____
- Has a debit card and can use it responsibly (follow-up supervision required) _____
- Has a prepaid credit card as the training for the temptation of plastic in their pocket (close supervision required and minimal prepaid limits on the card come from the child's savings account or earnings—parents do not prepay the card) _____
- Can manage and balance a clothing budget and personal financial budget _____
- Regularly reviews their personal financial budget with parents _____
- Regularly works inside and outside of the home during breaks from school _____
- Keeps a neat room and car _____
- Has paid one-third to one-half the cost of their car _____

- Pays insurance if they get a ticket or have an
  accident (parents can pay if they keep their
  driving record spotless)   _____
- Maintains a good GPA (or what they are
  capable of)   _____
- Has a regular volunteer position (hospital,
  coaching, church involvement, etc.)   _____
- Has a good grasp of delayed gratification   _____

Give yourself a pat on the back for loving your child enough to work through this chapter and give some thought to helping them have a full, stable, more peaceful adult life by knowing how to manage their finances. You're off to a great start!

CHAPTER ELEVEN

College Crunches
*How to Help Your Kids and Still Keep
Your Future*

I heard the sound of a child crying. It sounded like it was coming from the back of the house. I walked down the hall and looked into the boys' room. No one was there. I continued on to my daughter's room. When I opened the door, I found five-year-old Bethany sobbing into her pillow. Crying wasn't terribly unusual for our "Bunny," as she could have starred in a movie called "I Was a Preschool Drama Queen." Even so, she was usually laughing and hopping for joy, but when she had an occasional bad day, the rest of the family just about had to head for the hills!

"What's wrong, Bunny-rabbit?" I asked as I stroked her hair and braced for the drama.

"Well . . . it's . . . just—" she tried to catch her breath—"it's just . . . it's just that—" her tiny frame shook as she tried to compose herself—"I'm going to . . . (whimper) to go away to *college*!" At this, her sobbing started all over again.

Apparently she had a friend whose much older sibling just graduated from high school and was headed off to college. So Bethany deduced that when she "graduated" from kindergarten, we were going to ship her off to school!

$ $ $

Well, fast-forward almost a decade and we're already talking future college options with our "Middle-School Drama Queen." The majority of families say they want to send their children to college, but that same majority has very little means of paying for this dream—even those who are relatively debt free.

It's great to be rid of the extra baggage of debt. But if we're not careful, just like in food diets, it can be very easy for "debt weight" to creep back up on us. A primary way that debt sneaks up on parents is when they send a child to college. Many parents are thwarting their own future for their child's education. This chapter will offer practical tools to short-circuit these potentially debt-filled areas and keep your finances svelte and solid—even in the midst of those college years.

THE COLLEGE CRUNCH

For the 2003–2004 school year, the average tuition fee was $19,710 for a four-year private school and $4,694 for a four-year public school. These figures represent an increase of 6% and 14% over the preceding year and do not consider the pricey expense of room and board.

These amounts constitute a challenging prospect for parents who want to send their kids to an institution of higher learning. There is, however, good news where college costs are concerned if you are willing to do some homework, learn to save through tax-advantaged programs, look for low-cost educational loans, and find those golden eggs—college scholarships.

Your child's education shouldn't cost you your retirement.

First Things First

In any discussion of college costs, it's important to keep priorities straight. You should never borrow on *your* future in order to pay for your *child's* future. Your child's education shouldn't cost you your retirement. This means it's not a wise idea to take out a home equity loan, an equity line of credit, or to refinance your mortgage in order to pay for school. This would reduce the amount of equity in your home and increase the risk of possible foreclosure. You could also incur interest charges that may cost more if the term on the new mortgage is greater than the remaining term on the existing mortgage. For example, if you have ten years left on your mortgage, and you get a new 30-year loan, the length of time you will be paying on your home will greatly increase the interest you will have paid for your home, and the house payments will be there most likely when you are ready to retire. Furthermore, if you pull out enough money in equity to pay for the first year of college, you would need to do it again for the second year. If you pull out enough for four years of college, then you are paying interest on money that you won't need until the upcoming sophomore, junior, and senior years.

Savings Plans for Every Family

Saving for college is a highly individualized task. It will vary based on many different factors including your income level, number of children, amount of savings in existence, and the number of years left before your child starts college. Here's a guide to the most popular investment tools:

UGMA—Uniform Gifts to Minors Act: If you have a young child, start saving now for education but do it the tax-smart way. If you invest in the UGMA in your child's name, then the income is taxed at the child's marginal tax bracket rather than yours. The account must be registered in the child's name. An adult (usually a parent or grandparent) serves as custodian and is responsible for investing and managing the assets. But the child is the "beneficial owner," meaning the assets really belong to the child. At age eighteen (in most states), control of the assets must be turned over to the child (which could be a disadvantage for this plan).

All states offer UGMAs, and many have adopted the Uniform Transfers to Minors Act, or UTMA, as well. The former allows children to own stocks, bonds, mutual funds, and other securities; the latter also allows children to own real estate. Under UTMA, you can delay giving the assets to the child until age twenty-one.

According to Jeff Schnepper, of *MSN Money*, "If your two-year-old son has interest income of $700, the tax on that is zero. If he had income of $1,400, the next $700 is taxed at his 10% rate. If you're in the 30% bracket in 2002, the tax on the $1,400 total would be $420. Your son is only paying $70, so you've just saved $350 more for his college education."

EE U.S. Savings Bonds: If the income from these bonds is used to pay for education expenses, that interest may be excluded from taxes. But this exclusion is phased out beyond certain income levels.

Zero-Coupon Bonds: The interest on these bonds is deferred until they mature, when it is paid in a lump sum. You do have to pay income tax on interest as it accrues each year the bond is held. You could "ladder" these bonds so that they mature in every year of the child's college career.

529 Plan: This is an education savings plan operated by a state or educational institution designed to help families set aside funds for future college costs. As long as the plan satisfies a few basic requirements, the federal tax law provides special tax benefits to you, the plan participant (section 529 of the Internal Revenue Code). These 529 plans are usually categorized as either prepaid or savings, although some have elements of both. Every state now has at least one 529 plan available. It's up to each state to decide whether it will offer a 529 plan (or possibly more than one), and what it will look like. Educational institutions can offer a 529 prepaid plan but not a 529 savings plan (the private-college Independent 529 Plan is the only institution-sponsored 529 plan thus far). You can invest in any state's plan, no matter where you live, and regardless of what plan you choose, your beneficiary can attend any college or university in the country. What's more, grandparents or other benefactors can contribute money to a 529 plan. However, they may crimp financial aid in the future by increasing your and your student's assets.

Coverdell Education Savings Accounts: This "education IRA" will allow up to $2,000 of pre-tax income to be invested annually. There are limits on how much can be invested based on income, and the funds must be spent before the child turns thirty. This education IRA will not interfere with the parents' ability to invest in a $3,000 tax-deferred annuity in your own retirement account. But it will count heavily against the student when financial aid packages are calculated.

Jay Stillman, a consultant for Saving for College.com, says, "Because Coverdell IRA funds can be rolled over into a 529 without penalty, parents can sidestep its principal drawbacks—the age limit and the fact that the IRA counts as the child's asset, which can adversely affect his ability to receive need-based loans." Stillman goes on to say that a Coverdell account may be the best single investment option for parents whose income is below $50,000. The accounts are easier and less expensive to set up than 529 plans, and people in this lower tax bracket aren't usually able to take advantage of the maximum lifetime contributions allowed under a 529 because they don't pay that much tax in the first place.

Prepaid Tuition Plans: These are offered by individual states, and they are prepaid similarly to a 529 plan but are less risky. They allow parents to pay tomorrow's expenses at today's prices, either by the year or by the credit hour. The drawbacks are that even though you can often transfer some of these plans to other state colleges or private tuitions, those schools do not guarantee the same services and prices. Thus you could come up short. Contributions to prepaid plans might also reduce a student's eligibility for financial aid on a dollar-to-dollar basis, more than with a 529 plan. If the child does not attend college, the contributions are refundable but there might be a cancellation fee and/or loss of interest earned. These plans are best if (1) you don't expect to qualify for financial aid; (2) you're a conservative or novice investor; and (3) you understand the risks.

Financial Aid Office: The university's financial aid office is a clearinghouse of information. A good aid office will not only help students determine what loans they qualify for, but they will steer them to participating lenders who are offering the best terms and service. Parents can do their own assessment at *www.collegeboard.com* by clicking onto *For Parents*, then *Paying for College*, and accessing the calculator tool.

The FASFA (Free Application for Student Financial Aid form) is the first step in applying for aid, including: (1) need-based guaranteed loans (Stafford loans are variable and currently at 3.42%, while Perkins loans are at a fixed 5%); (2) grants—the Pell Grant and the federal Supplemental Education Opportunity Grant each provide a gift of up to $4,050 per student per student year; (3) work-study. Students can receive up to $2,000 per year, 25% of it matched by the participating institution, from the federal work-study program.

There are also state loans and grants available, and the financial aid office should be able to quickly assess the student's eligibility.

Scholarships: Millions of dollars of scholarship money goes unclaimed every year. This is free-lunch money that parents or prospective students who are willing to do some detective work may find more quickly than they think. Go to the *www.fastweb.com* search engine to get started, and don't forget scholarships offered by your local civic organizations. Your high school counselor should have a list of these scholarships.

How Much College Debt Is Too Much?

As mentioned in our discussion of mortgages, there are two kinds of debt: what is commonly known as "good" debt and "bad" debt, with student loans qualified as the former. So what's the problem? Well, four years of loans can last a lifetime if you're not careful. Many students are now $30,000 to $40,000 in debt from student loans by the time they graduate. If they can't find work in their fields, they are in big trouble. Even if a student graduates with the average debt load of $18,000, they may be jeopardizing their finances by servicing the debt and putting off other goals, such as funding an IRA or saving for a house.

For example, if a twenty-two-year-old contributes $3,000 to a Roth IRA, it would grow to around $95,000 by the time she's eligible for social security. But if she has to put off that contribution by ten years because she's servicing student loans, then her gain will only be half as large, or $44,000, by the time she hits retirement. It is up to you as to how much debt you are willing to accumulate. As in the cases of credit card and mortgage debt—lenders are willing to lend you far more than you can comfortably repay.

Even though federal law limits the amount of student loans, the government will lend to any given student; private institutions do not have such limitations, and that is where students or their parents get into trouble. Lenders have a reasonable belief that they will get their money back because it's not as easy to walk away from these student loans as it used to be. There are ways to track down defaulters, and these loans are usually not erased in bankruptcy proceedings.

So how much can you safely borrow? Here are several points to help you decide what your debt threshold should be:

- *Ten Percent of Salary Rule*—You need to research what the entry level position of your career field will pay once you graduate. You should never borrow more than 10% of your expected gross pay per college year.
- *Thirty-Five Percent Debt Rule*—If you are a parent, all your debts—including your mortgage, consumer debt, car loans, and education loans should not consume more than 35% of your gross pay.
- *Eight-Percent Interest Rule*—On variable rate loans it is best to figure the debt at 8% interest because when rates go up they will be capped between 8.25% and 9% (depending on the lender and type of loan). At 8% each $1,000 you borrow will cost you about $12/month to repay, assuming a ten-year loan. If you're a student and borrow the maximum allowed under the federal student loan programs (a qualified $23,000), the payment will be $276.
- *Tracking Rule*—Once you begin to borrow on student loans, keep track of your debt. If you are borrowing from several different lending institutions, and since you will not have to begin repaying some loans until after graduation, it's easy to get confused about how much you owe.

If students borrow the maximum amount, they will need to make at least $33,000 per year, which means they had better consider a career in accounting or business, because starting salaries in those fields currently range from around $36,000 for a business administrator to $43,000 for management information systems personnel. Otherwise, they could have a difficult time paying off student loans when they get their first job.

A liberal arts major, for example, would more than likely have to settle for an initial salary under $30,000, and psychology majors start out at $26,000, while an English major's starting salary would be around $28,000. At those lower pay levels, you should keep your debt level well below $12,000 ($3,000 per year for four years) in order to make ends meet after graduation. To find the starting salary in your field on the Internet, just type "starting salary for _____" into any search engine.

According to Liz Pulliam Weston, *MSN Money* columnist:

> Parents, too, need to put limits on their borrowing, since too much debt can keep them from adequately funding their other goals such as saving for retirement. . . . Parents also should avoid the temptation to tap all their home equity to pay for a child's college education. If you borrow more than 80% of the value of your home, including your first mortgage, you pay higher interest rates and have little cushion left for emergencies.

Once you've decided how much you can comfortably borrow, do not use more than 15% to 20% of it the first year. College costs tend to rise in consecutive years, and most lenders estimate that you will need two-thirds of the total student loan amount to cover the last two years of school. As an example of these rising costs, you could look at the maximum amounts allowed by the Stafford student loans. The first year limit is $2,625, the second year is $3,600, and the last two years are maxed out at $5,500.

Low-Cost Alternatives

Sometimes, no matter how you do the math, you're still going to come up short for college costs, so here are five final tips to keep in mind:

- *Who Wants You?*—Besides Uncle Sam, there may be some other institution that "wants you" for their school. First consider the colleges that are recruiting you, because they are more likely to give you a better financial aid package.

- *Two-Year Transfer*—You could opt to go to a lower-cost school or junior college the first two years and then transfer. Your degree will have the name of the university from which you graduated, and you will have saved the higher costs of the first two years. You must, however, make sure that your credits will transfer before you pursue this route.

- *High School Credits*—There are some states that allow students to receive college credits for courses they take in high school. If your school offers this, and students work extra hard, they could conceivably get an associate degree at the same time they receive their high school degree.

- *CLEP*—The "College-Level Examination Program" provides students of any age with the opportunity to demonstrate college-level achievement through a program of exams in undergraduate college courses. There are 2,900 colleges that grant credit and/or advanced standing for CLEP exams. Find out more at *www.collegeboard.com*. This allows you to save time and money and get credit for what you already know. Personally, I CLEPped out of fourteen credits for Spanish! *¿Cómo que no?*

- *Jobs*—A summer or part-time job is a great way for students to "own" part of their college education. Our oldest daughter, Missy, not only participated in a work-study program at Columbia University, but she also took a year off between her sophomore and junior years to work. She feels very proud of her degree because she *earned* it in every way.

FISCAL FITNESS WORKOUT

SURF YOUR WAY TO COLLEGE SAVINGS

Maybe this section has inspired you to take some steps toward providing for your own or your child's college education. Here are some nifty Internet tools that can get you started on your adventure of saving for college.

Tuition Savings Calculation Tool: This will allow you to calculate how much you will need for college based on your child's age and your current savings patterns (*www.moneycentral. msn.com/investor/calcs/n_college/main.asp*).

Paying for College: Go to the parents' page at *www. collegeboard.com* and learn about college costs, applying for scholarships and other types of financial aid, choosing the best aid package, taking out education loans, and paying the college bill.

Scholarship Search Wizard: This site (*http://fast-web.monster.com/cpt/*) is a great place to learn about your financial aid options for college. FastWeb's scholarship search will automatically match available scholarships to your personal profile.

For many awards, you can apply right online (look for the "Apply Online" icon). FastWeb will e-mail updates to keep you posted as new scholarships become available.

"The 100 Best Values in Public College": This helpful list can be found at *www.kiplinger.com/tools/colleges/*. You can sort the schools in the survey of public colleges by in-state and out-of-state, overall rank, cost, quality measures, or financial aid measures. Clicking on the college names in the table will take you to the individual college Web sites.

Saving for College Guides: Go to *www.savingforcollege.com* to find the Internet guide to 529 plans for your state, Coverdell ESA, and college-planning resources.

Good luck and happy hunting. There are a lot of possibilities out there, and *you* are just the one to find the best.

CHAPTER TWELVE

Visiting the Spa

The "Treat" of Shopping to Share

As we made our way toward the grocery store checkout, my eleven-year-old, Jonathan, said, "Can I go through the line and buy my things by myself?"

I looked down at my freckle-faced boy. His eyes were bright with excitement. He was buying groceries for his sister and her new husband to help the newlyweds set up the pantry in their first home.

"Sure, son," I quickly agreed. "I'll be here when you're done."

After a few minutes I heard a commotion in Jonathan's lane. The store manager, the checker, and a sacker were engaged in excited conversation with my son as he was paying his bill.

When Jonathan finished, he proudly held three grocery bags. As he approached me, I asked, "Honey, what happened over there?"

He smiled broadly, "My total before coupons was $28.60, but afterward it was only $1.80! They had a hard time believing I could save that much!"

If an eleven-year-old can learn to save money in the grocery store, so can you! Our family saved over $8,000 last year on food, toiletries, and cleaning products. That is the equivalent of

$13,500 *earned* when deductions for social security and taxes are factored in. Consequently, a penny saved can be *more* than a penny earned.

But we can learn more from this eleven-year-old than how to save money. He is also a wonderful case study in what we can do with the money we save. He used coupons solely for the benefit of someone else, which on this occasion happened to be his newlywed sister and her husband.

Well-known financial experts (Suze Orman, David Bach, Jean Sherman Chatsky, and Dave Ramsey) advocate the use of a "tithe" or giving in some way to others on a regular basis from your income.

In general, the more money a person makes the less likely he/she is to tithe. "While 8% of those making $20,000 or less gave at least 10% of their income to churches, that proportion dropped to 5% among those in the $20,000–$29,999 and $30,000–$39,999 categories; to 4% among those in the $40,000–$59,999 range, down to 2% for those in the $60,000–$74,999 niche; and to 1% for those making $75,000–$99,999. The level jumped a bit for those making $100,000 or more, as 5% of the most affluent group tithed in 1999" (George Barna news release by Barna Research Group, April 5, 2000, *www.generousgiving.org*). Sometimes little guys, like Jonathan, lead the way in showing us how to develop a mindset of saving to share.

After we look at some specific ways to save in the grocery store, we're going to also review ways to share with those who need our generosity.

Seven Savings Factors

There are basically seven "Savings Factors" that can be used to save money in the grocery store. The more of these factors you combine, the more likely you are to get items for pennies or even for free.

STORE CARDS

These are sometimes referred to as "clipless coupons." Sign up for the card at the customer service desk and as it is scanned at the checkout, you will receive any or all of the store's special values for the week that appear in your cart.

SALE ADS

The following smooth move is something you probably saw your mom perform when you were growing up. She pored over the local grocery stores' weekly ads that came either in the newspaper or the mail and may even have made stops at several stores to save money on the grocery bill. Today, coupons and special offers are far more plentiful than in Mom's day. Match up the sale ads you receive with some of the other savings factors listed below and you'll soon find yourself buying products for pennies.

MANUFACTURER'S COUPONS

These are traditional coupons issued and reimbursed by the manufacturer. If you read the fine print of the coupon, you'll see the manufacturer's name and mailing address. Here are a few places to find these coupons:

- *FSIs (Free-Standing Inserts)*—Most of these are found in

the Sunday paper. You might want to purchase multiple copies of the newspaper in order to get more FSIs.

- *Shelf Coupon Dispensers*—These are the light-blinking dispensers in the grocery store aisle that disperse coupons for your convenience. Most shelf coupons cannot be doubled at a double coupon store.
- *Products*—Some products have coupons right on them that you can tear off and use immediately. Others require that you purchase the item to find the coupons inside the box or to cut them out from the packaging.
- *Electronic*—These coupons are issued at the checkout after you've purchased your groceries. They are usually competitor coupons that are automatically issued as a result of your choices. For example, last week I bought Quaker Toaster Treats™ (for 60 cents a box with three different savings factors) and I received an electronic coupon for 50 cents off Pop-Tarts.™

DOUBLE COUPONS

Some stores offer "double" (or "triple") coupons. This is where the coupon is worth twice the face value—so a 50-cent coupon is now worth $1. There are limitations issued by the store, such as "only double up to $1" or "double coupons limited to three like items." So check the customer-service desk for details. Go to the links page at *elliekay.com* to find a link listing all the stores that double coupons in your state. If you want to introduce double coupons to your area, go to the chapter called "Coupon Cheerleaders" in my book *How to Save Money Every Day*, or e-mail *wendywendler@elliekay.com* for the attachment by the same name.

Store Coupons

A true store coupon is issued by the store and reimbursed by the store's marketing department. It will either have the store's mailing address or it may not have an address and only the store name. A true store coupon can be combined with a manufacturer's coupon on the same item. For example, at Walgreens Drugstore, there was a store coupon for Secret deodorant for 99 cents, and I had a manufacturer's coupon for $1 off any Secret. When I combined these two savings factors, the deodorant was free. Read the fine print before you try to combine offers.

Unadvertised Sales and Clearances

Check the store aisles for sales and clearance tags. As much as 50% of the week's sales are not advertised. When you begin to get these products free through the combined savings of clearance prices and coupons, you'll be able to share them with those in need.

WebBucks or ValuPage

If you go to *www.valupage* (no "e" on valu), you'll find links to participating stores. When items on this list are purchased, you will automatically get coupons good for cash off your next shopping trip. I once went shopping in front of the television cameras for *Good Morning, Texas* in Dallas, and the total before coupons was $127. After coupons, I paid $22 and received $20 in WebBucks that could be used on my next trip. If you use coupons from these ValuPage items, you'll save even more.

As you shop, be sure to keep a "sharing"
mindset so that you can be a blessing
to someone in the community.

When you go to the store, especially during the holidays, there will be many opportunities to combine these savings factors and get groceries for a dime on the dollar. Don't forget that often you may be God's provision for someone else in need. So as you shop, be sure to keep a "sharing" mindset so that you can be a blessing to someone in the community.

FISCAL FITNESS WORKOUT

SETTING GOALS FOR SAVINGS

As I've said before, there's an old saying in Texas: "If you aim at nothing, you'll hit it every time." It's important to have a family meeting and decide what you'll do with your savings and what nonprofit groups you want to share with. Here are some ideas to help you get started:

Immediate Savings: You might want to write a check to a special savings account for the amount you are saving in the store. That way it won't get absorbed back into the family spending.

Pay Down Debt: Why not take the $20 you saved this week and immediately write another check to your credit card company to start paying down your debt? Every time you pay more than your minimum, you improve your FICO score (credit rating). Families who follow the "workouts" and disciplines of *The Debt Diet* are becoming debt free by channeling their savings toward this area.

Cash for Cars: Other families have set up a goal of paying cash for a second car. They diligently put the "saved" money aside and within a year they're able to buy a vehicle—debt free.

Dream Vacations: Some families put their money into a dream vacation account for a trip to Hawaii, Europe, or a theme park—with no accumulated debt.

Missions: You might consider "adopting" a third-world child through WorldVision.org or Compassion.com, two excellent organizations that bring food, clothing, housing, education, and the Good News to children around the world.

Positive Problems

I'd like to close this book by sharing a different perspective on your debt. Sometimes our problems can be our salvation—or the salvation of others. When Bob and I had $40,000 of consumer debt and had to eat groceries given to us by his former mother-in-law, I couldn't see how that kind of "problem" could ever be construed as "positive."

But life has a way of turning the tables on us. We persevered, trying to do the right thing to get out of debt and still be generous in the journey. It led to the opportunity for me to conduct seminars, write books, and eventually appear on television, sharing this wonderful discovery with others.

A few years ago I had the chance to be part of a national television show's annual "Feed the Hungry" fund-raising campaign. The goal was to feed one million people a day in the ravaged country of Somalia. The host and producers decided to put me on the air every day that week. I remember feeling so inadequate to the task, wishing that the host would just do the fund-raising by himself.

I had a talk with God about it and pleaded, "Why me? I'm just a mom. Why not send someone more qualified, like the host or a celebrity?" Although I didn't hear an audible voice, a thought immediately came to me as real as the person sitting next to me. "You must do this because people will respond more to someone they can relate to than to a celebrity."

By the end of the week a new record had been set for their "Feed the Hungry" TV campaign, and as a result over one million people would have food to eat in Somalia. I imagined a sea of dark faces, singing and dancing for joy that their children would have clothing, medical supplies, and food—and a chance to live.

Who would have thought way back when Bob and I were struggling like crazy to pay down our $40K-debt that one day, our "problem" would be turned around to help save the lives of one million strangers in a faraway land.

I deeply believe we have the ability to be free from debt and also free from the bondage of living in the shadow of our past problems. You never know what positive outcome today's problems could have tomorrow. So I would encourage you to embrace them, work through them, and let them one day become the wisdom whereby you can serve others.

I believe that we are blessed so that we can be a blessing to someone else. I believe our blessings can have the greater destiny of impacting others for good.

$ $ $

Okay everybody, got your running shoes on? Let's slim down, shape up, and laugh all the way to the bank—remembering to stop by the food pantry or help someone in need with all the free stuff we earned from our savvy savings strategies.

My desire for you is that you will experience not only the joy of removing the weight of your debt, but the elation of helping others as you journey along the way to your goal.

Recommended Resources

Recommended Resources by Ellie Kay Found at *www.elliekay.com*:

A Woman's Guide to Family Finances, Bethany House Publishers, 2004. This is a guide that every woman should have in order to know how to manage household finances and how to help her family achieve financial freedom.

Heroes at Home, Bethany House Publishers, 2003. This book was a Gold Medallion Book Award finalist. It helps military families cope with their sometimes hectic and challenging lifestyle. From learning how to move smarter to the unique financial matters military families face to coping with separations, this book has it all.

How to Save Money Every Day, Bethany House Publishers, 2001. This is a guide to help you save on absolutely everything—from cars to utilities to household goods.

Money Doesn't Grow on Trees, Bethany House Publishers, 2002. This book guides parents in how to teach their children about money matters. From tips for toddlers to college-bound kids, this comprehensive book helps prepare the future generation to be ready for financial matters.

The New Bride Guide, Bethany House Publishers, 2003. This book not only helps the bride plan the wedding, reception, and honeymoon on a budget, but it also deals with topics that arise in the first year of marriage—from budgets to in-laws to communication and intimacy, this is a definitive guide for the new bride.

Recommended Resources Found at *www.crown.org*:

The Personal Finances Package includes *How to Manage Your Money* and the *Family Financial Workbook* by Larry Burkett, $25 (Moody Publishers, 2001).

The Organizer Package includes the newly updated Cash Organizer™ and the Bill Organizer™, $23.

Cash Organizer™

The newly revised and updated Cash Organizer™ envelope budgeting system will simplify your budgeting plan by keeping you in control of your cash spending. It will hold you accountable by budget category—if there's no money left in a particular envelope, you're finished spending in that category until payday! Twelve tear-resistant envelopes neatly keep each category organized in a durable navy blue expanding file. The Cash Organizer™ also comes with pre-printed category stickers, a handy ledger booklet for recording your transactions, and a practical teaching pamphlet on managing your money according to biblical principles.

Bill Organizer™

With the Bill Organizer,™ there's no more searching frantically for that misplaced phone bill or wondering if the power bill has been paid! This expanding file of durable green plastic contains twelve tabbed pockets that can be customized easily to organize your bills by either category or due date!

Pre-printed stickers and ledger sheets for tracking your payments are included. Also included with your Bill Organizer™ purchase is Larry Burkett's helpful audiotape "Taking Charge of Your Credit Card." He gives a history of the use and misuse of credit in our society and then provides steps to help you:

(1) gain control of your credit spending; and

(2) avoid falling into the debt trap ever again.

Recommended Resources Found at Ronald Blue and Company, LLC *www.ronaldblue.com*:

Master Your Money by Ron Blue. This bestselling book explains the biblical principles of personal finance and stewardship combined with application in today's financial world. Published by Thomas Nelson (1997).

Generous Living by Ron Blue. This book explains why an open-handed spirit is the key to freedom, contentment, and joy. Ron Blue helps you start cultivating a generous lifestyle right where you are and shows you what happens when you become a giver. *Generous Living* will point you beyond guilt-induced giving and show you the true way to give effectively, joyfully, and wisely. Published by Zondervan (1997).

Raising Money-Smart Kids by Ron Blue. Based on the belief that parenting includes not only a huge financial investment but also the investment of spiritual wealth, this book teaches parents how to train their children to be good stewards. Published by Thomas Nelson (1992).

Money Talks and So Can We by Ron & Judy Blue. The Blues insist that marital problems are never about money, but about communication. This book will aid couples in talking openly and honestly about money as well as operating like a team. Advice on effective communication, setting monetary priorities, evaluating the pros and cons of dual-income households, and many more insights are included. Published by Zondervan (1999).

Glossary of Terms

Account Agreement: The account terms that apply to your credit card account. The agreement states your annual percentage rates, account fees, payment calculation method, rights in billing disputes, and account terms and conditions.

Annual Fee: The yearly fee that may be charged to maintain the credit card account.

Annual Percentage Rate (APR): The cost of credit, expressed as a yearly rate.

Annual Percentage Yield (APY): The amount paid to customers as interest on their savings deposit. This is a term associated with savings accounts.

Authorized User: A person permitted by the account holder to use the account. Authorized users are subject to the same credit line. The account holder is responsible for any charges made by the authorized user.

Available Credit: The amount of unused credit on an account. You can check your available credit by calling your credit card company's Customer Service.

Average Daily Balance: The average daily balance is calculated by adding each day's balances together and then dividing the sum by the number of days within the cycle for the current month.

Balance: The total amount of credit you have spent on purchases, cash advances, and balance transfers, plus finance charges and fees.

Balance Transfer: The movement of the balance of one credit card account to another credit card account.

Billing Cycle: The period of time between billing statements. A billing cycle is typically thirty days, but because of weekends, holidays, and the variance in the number of days in a month, a billing cycle may be somewhat shorter or longer.

Business Days: The days that most companies are open to conduct business. Monday through Friday, except bank holidays, are generally considered business days.

Calendar Days: The seven days of the calendar week. Every day is considered a calendar day.

Cash Advance: Using a credit card to withdraw cash from an ATM or bank, or other methods described in the Account Agreement, such as checks sent to you. Cash advances are subtracted from the available credit and become part of the cash advance balance. There may be only a portion of your credit line available for cash advances.

Cash Advance Fee: A charge assessed for taking a cash advance.

Compounding Interest: Interest on an investment (for example, a savings account) that is calculated not only on the money you originally invested but also on any interest the investment has already earned.

Co-signer: This is a credit-worthy individual, usually a parent or spouse, who signs a credit agreement and is legally obligated to take responsibility for loan repayment if the principal borrower fails to do so.

Credit Bureau: An institution that collects and reports facts about your credit history. These facts are then compiled into a "credit report," which can be accessed by potential lenders, employers, etc. The three major credit reporting agencies are Equifax, Experian, and TransUnion.

Credit Line (or Credit Limit): The amount of credit being extended to you by a bank (often via a credit card) to make purchases, cash advances, and other transactions.

Credit Line Increase: An increase in the amount of the credit line.

Credit Rating (or Credit Score): A calculation based on one's personal credit history, provided by credit bureaus to lenders, that helps predict future credit performance.

Credit Report: A record of all the information that a credit bureau has collected about the way you have managed your credit accounts over time. It includes your lenders, your current account records, and the timeliness of your payments. The information on your credit report may be used when you apply for credit cards, mortgages, other loans, car or apartment leases, and possibly employment.

Cycle Date: The date on which a billing period ends and a new billing period begins.

Delinquency: A payment that is overdue.

Dispute: A process through which you can request to review unauthorized charges and remove them from your account.

Due Date: The date by which a payment must be received before the account is considered late and a late fee is charged.

Equifax (formerly Credit Bureau Incorporated): One of the three major credit bureaus.

Experian (formerly TRW): One of the three major credit bureaus.

Expiration Date: The last day of the designated month/year the credit card is valid. (This date is imprinted on the credit card.)

Fair Credit Reporting Act: A consumer protection law that regulates the disclosure of consumer credit reports by credit reporting agencies and establishes procedures for correcting mistakes on a person's credit record.

FICO: Your credit score, calculated from data in your credit report, which lenders use to rate your credit risk. This is called "FICO" because most credit bureau scores use formulas developed by Fair Isaac Corporation®.

Finance Charge: The cost of credit, more commonly referred to as "interest."

Fraudulent Activity: Transactions on your account not made by you or someone you permit to use your card.

Grace Period on Purchases: A feature of some credit card accounts that allows an interest-free period of time between the transaction date of the purchase and the billing date. If there is no grace period, finance charges will accrue immediately when a purchase is made with the credit card.

HELOC: Home Equity Line of Credit—a secure line of credit using the available equity in your residence as collateral.

Home Equity Loan: Sometimes referred to as a second mortgage or borrowing against your home. This loan allows you to tap into your home's built-up equity (the difference between the amount your home could be sold for and the amount you still owe) to finance home improvements, refinance other debt, etc. Home equity loans have low interest rates and the interest is usually tax-deductible; however, they also reduce the amount of equity in your home and increase the risk of possible foreclosure, as the lender can take possession of your home if the loan isn't repaid.

Household Income: The total income of all members of a household. The income can come from many sources, including wages, commissions, bonuses, alimony, child support, social security/retirement benefits, unemployment compensation, or disability, dividends, and interest. Income from alimony, child support, or separate maintenance payments need not be disclosed unless you want it considered in determining your creditworthiness.

Issuer: The banking institution that issues the credit card.

Joint Account: A financial account for which two people are both responsible for paying the balance on the account.

Late Fee: The fee charged to your account if your minimum monthly credit card payment does not reach your lender by the due date on your payment coupon. Your payment must be received by that date to be on time.

Minimum Payment: The smallest amount of your balance you can pay by the due date and still meet the terms of your Account Agreement. You can always pay more than your minimum payment. Your minimum payment can vary from month to month based on your current balance.

Nonsufficient Funds (NSF): When a check is returned because there are not enough funds in a checking account.

Overdraft Protection: A service offered by financial institutions that ensures all checks and withdrawals are covered regardless of whether adequate funds are available in the account. This service will typically involve a fee and be limited to a preset maximum amount. Interest is usually charged on the overdraft until it is repaid.

Overlimit: The amount of your balance that exceeds your credit limit. If this occurs, you may be charged an overlimit fee.

Past Due: The status of an account when the minimum payment has not been received by the due date.

Personal Identification Number (PIN): A secret number that is mailed to you that allows you to use your credit or debit cards at ATMs.

Post Date: The date when the cash advance, purchase, or payment is processed by the lender.

Prime Rate: A banking index that is published on every day of every month in *The Wall Street Journal*. Many variable APRs are tied to the prime rate.

Revolving Credit: A credit agreement (typically a credit card) that allows a customer to borrow against a preapproved credit line when purchasing goods and services. The borrower is only billed for the amount that is actually borrowed, plus any interest due, and may pay all or part of the outstanding balance. As credit is paid off, it becomes available again to use for another purchase or cash advance.

Statement: A summary that itemizes your charges and credits. It includes the minimum payment due on your account and the due date.

Transaction Date: The actual date that a cash advance is taken, a purchase is made, or payment is credited to the account.

TransUnion: One of the three major credit bureaus.

Wire Transfer: A transfer of funds electronically from an account in one banking institution to an account in another banking institution.

Get a kick out of sharing

You can put a soccer ball in the hands of a needy child around the world! Participate in our **Get A Kick Out of Sharing** program and you'll be joining a nationwide effort to obtain donations of 250,000 new and gently used soccer balls for children in need.

Children love soccer. Many have only rounded wads of trash or rag balls to kick and play with. They have never played with a real ball.

You can share the joy of soccer and give these children hope by being a Get A Kick Out of Sharing teammate. Cash gifts enable the purchase of new balls and cover the costs of transporting the balls to needy children worldwide. **In fact, a gift of just $50 will provide soccer balls for five children.**

To make your contribution go even further, check to see if your employer will match your donation. Your human resources department can tell you if your company offers matching donations and if World Vision is an eligible recipient. If so, complete the form below and send it to World Vision along with a completed matching gift form (provided by your employer).

For more information, call
1.800.642.1616 today, or visit www.worldvision.org/soccerballs

30382_0303

Yes, I want to help!

Rush this coupon with your cash gift to:
World Vision • P.O. Box 9716 • MS 442
Federal Way, WA 98063-9716
Get A Kick Out of Sharing!

☐ I am donating _____ soccer ball(s). Please deflate and ship your soccer ball(s) to:
World Vision, International Distribution Center—Soccer Balls
210 Overlook Drive, 79 North Industrial Park, Sewickley, PA 15143

Please accept my cash donation of:

☐ $50 to provide soccer balls for 5 children.
☐ $150 to provide soccer balls for 15 children.
☐ $500 to provide soccer balls for 50 children.
☐ Other: $_____ (indicate amount)

☐ I would like my gift to be matched by my company. Please see attached form.
☐ Please send me more information about the "Get A Kick Out of Sharing" program.

☐ Check (please make payable to World Vision)
☐ Please bill my credit card: ☐ VISA ☐ MasterCard ☐ American Express ☐ Discover

Card No. _____ Exp. Date _____

Name on Card _____

Signature (required) _____

NAME

ADDRESS

CITY   STATE   ZIP

DAY PHONE   FAX   E-MAIL

WV9906

More Crucial Financial Advice From
AMERICA'S
Family Financial Expert®

THE BOOK THAT STARTED IT ALL—
UPDATED FOR TODAY'S ECONOMY

Ellie Kay's core message has always been the same—find ways to save money so that you can have more to share with others. This book, newly updated to address lean economic times, packs easy-to-follow advice into every page.

Shop, Save, and Share

FINANCIAL BASICS EVERY WOMAN NEEDS TO KNOW

Discover the information you need to know to play your part in managing a fiscally responsible household, which will increase your confidence and prepare you for any emergency. These are essential tips for saving real money in this unreal economy.

A Woman's Guide to Family Finances